Successful

Kindergarten

Transition

Successful

Kindergarten

Transition

Your Guide to
Connecting
Children,
Families,
& Schools

Robert C. Pianta, Ph.D.
Marcia Kraft-Sayre, L.C.S.W.

National Center for Early Development & Learning
University of Virginia, Charlottesville

·P A U L ·H·
BROOKES
PUBLISHING CO®

Baltimore • London • Sydney

Paul H. Brookes Publishing Co.
Post Office Box 10624
Baltimore, Maryland 21285-0624

www.brookespublishing.com

Typeset by Typeshoppe II, Chestertown, Maryland.
Manufactured in the United States of America by
Versa Press, East Peoria, Illinois.

The work reported here was under the Educational Research and Development Centers
Program, PR/Award Number R307A60004, as administered by the Office of Educational
Research and Improvement, U.S. Department of Education. The contents do not necessarily
represent the positions or policies of the National Institute on Early Childhood Development
and Education, the Office of Education Sciences, or the U.S. Department of Education, and
readers should not assume endorsement by the federal government.

Second printing, October 2003.

Library of Congress Cataloging-in-Publication Data

Pianta, Robert C.
   Successful kindergarten transition: Your guide to connecting children, families, and schools /
      by Robert C. Pianta and Marcia Kraft-Sayre.
         p.   cm.
   Includes bibliographical references and index.
      ISBN 1-55766-615-6
      1. Kindergarten—United States.   2. Education, Preschool—United States.   I. Kraft-Sayre,
      Marcia.   II. Title.
LB1205.P53 2003
372.21'8—dc21

                                                                              2003044306

British Library Cataloguing in Publication data are available from the British Library.

Contents

About the Authors

Robert C. Pianta, Ph.D., is Professor in the Curry School of Education's Programs in Clinical and School Psychology at the University of Virginia and holds the William Clay Parrish Jr. Chair in Education. A former special education teacher, he is a developmental, school, and clinical child psychologist whose work focuses on how children's experiences at home and in school affect their development. He is particularly interested in how relationships with teachers and parents, as well as classroom quality, can help improve outcomes for children and youth who are at risk. Dr. Pianta is Principal Investigator on the National Institute of Child Health and Human Development Study of Early Child Care and Youth Development, Senior Investigator with the National Center for Early Development & Learning (NCEDL), and Editor of the *Journal of School Psychology.* He is the author of more than 100 journal articles, chapters, and books in the areas of early childhood development, school readiness, and parent–child and teacher–child relationships, and he consults regularly with several foundations, universities, and federal agencies.

Marcia Kraft-Sayre, L.C.S.W., is Regional Project Coordinator for the National Center for Early Development & Learning (NCEDL) Multi-State Study of Pre-Kindergarten at the University of Virginia. She has also served as Coordinator for the NCEDL Kindergarten Transition Project. Her current work entails managing data collection for a national study of state-funded pre-kindergarten programs. She is the co-author of several articles about the transition to kindergarten. For 15 years prior to coming to NCEDL, she worked as a clinical social worker with children and families in mental health and medical settings.

Preface

This book describes an approach to enhancing children's transitions into kindergarten. We developed the method and then implemented it through the collaborative efforts of researchers at the National Center for Early Development & Learning (NCEDL) Kindergarten Transition Project at the University of Virginia and school personnel in a variety of districts and states. The method focuses on forming a network of social and informational linkages that support children and families during the transition to school.

These linkages are important for supporting competencies in young children that can ensure their school success—they are resources for children. When social and informational connections are established and maintained, children may have more positive school experiences because more resources are available. For example, if parents have positive relationships with their children's teachers (a social linkage), then teachers and parents can work more effectively together to support children's educational progress. Similarly, when preschool providers and kindergarten teachers meet regularly to discuss how to integrate their curricula (an informational linkage), then children are more likely to be offered educational opportunities that smoothly connect with their prior experiences and skills. Also, peer relationships that continue from preschool and neighborhood experiences into kindergarten (another social connection) can help ease children's transition to school and function as avenues for building social competencies. Our approach systematically addresses the multiple connections that affect children's transition to school.

The book provides an approach that school districts and communities can use to generate, implement, and evaluate a transition plan that suits their needs. A variety of transition strategies are offered that can be tailored to the individual needs of families and schools. Good transition planning should not result in a "one size fits all" program applicable to *all* schools and *all* families. Every family's needs are different, and each community has unique characteristics and constraints. Rather, good transition planning offers a framework for enhancing children's transition into kindergarten that can include a range of practices that educators can use in their local settings.

The book describes this framework and our experiences in collaborating with local communities and states in developing and implementing interventions to smooth children's transition into kindergarten. Through the collaborative process, we learned firsthand about transition issues facing families and schools. We share what we learned from this collaboration, what school personnel and families say about successful strategies, and the challenges they face in the process. This guide includes quotations from teachers, administrators, and parents who were involved in our intervention that epitomize, capture, and clarify the material.

Chapter 1 describes several ways to think about transition with a focus on the model used in our approach (Rimm-Kaufman & Pianta, 1999). In addition, the key principles used in formulating a community transition plan are described. Chapter 2 outlines the components of a transition plan. Chapter 3 presents a menu of specific transition practices that communities can use to develop their own specific transition strategies. Chapter 4 discusses the process by which transition programs can be implemented, evaluated, and revised. Chapter 5 highlights our experiences in implementing this approach in a variety of settings. Chapter 6 focuses on what we learned in conducting this project and how this relates to the principles we used in designing the intervention. The Appendix contains examples of forms that transition teams can use or adapt in creating their own customized transition plans that meet the needs of children, families, and schools. Community and school transition teams can use this book—combined with a priority on collaboration and relationships, a common model of transition, and an emphasis on addressing local communities' and individuals' needs and goals—to help ensure that all children start school on the right foot!

REFERENCE

Rimm-Kaufman, S.E., & Pianta, R.C. (1999). Patterns of family–school contact in preschool and kindergarten. *School Psychology Review, 28*(3), 426–438.

Acknowledgments

This project could not have been undertaken without the generous support and effort of a number of people and organizations. Throughout the process, the project was supported by the U.S. Department of Education's funding of the National Center for Early Development & Learning (NCEDL). NCEDL investigators Martha Cox, Carollee Howes, Dick Clifford, Donna Bryant, Pam Winton, Peg Burchinal, and Diane Early all contributed ideas and support. The NCEDL director, Don Bailey, was instrumental in securing support for this project and in guiding us through early stages of the work. Naomi Karp, Director of the National Institute on Early Childhood Development and Education, the funding source for NCEDL, played a key role in providing financial and intellectual support for this work.

We were fortunate to work with a set of dedicated, skilled, and generous early childhood professionals who encouraged us to establish partnerships with them. Several school systems allowed us access to early childhood and school settings to explore our ideas about transition. We could not have done this work without the participating parents and teachers, whose insight and dedication are evident in this book. Also, key people were exceptionally generous with their time and insight. We extend our sincere thanks to Nancy Gercke, Terri Higgins, Jan Pandy, Sue Tansey, Donna Mendonca, Jane Crowell, and Enid Rey. Our colleagues Sara Rimm-Kaufman and Daniel Walsh played key roles in shaping the ideas that gave rise to the practices we describe here. We are grateful to them and to Jeanne Stovall and Aileen Walsh for their thorough and careful attention to many versions of this manuscript. Finally, we thank our collaborators at Paul H. Brookes Publishing Co. for their efforts.

A Developmental
Approach to
Transition

"Two weeks before school started, Nate's teacher called. It was great, [and it] made Nate feel great. What a nice thing to do!"

"The first week of school, the teacher called to say that my child should be evaluated for Ritalin."

These quotations from interviews with parents after their children's first 2 weeks of kindergarten reveal a variety of experiences and feelings. Nate's mother describes the school reaching out to her and to her son, making a personal connection, establishing a smooth transition, and finding out whether they needed anything to facilitate this move for Nate and his parents. This kind of connection paves the way for a resourceful and productive relationship between Nate's parents and his school that, if he has difficulties, can be drawn on to solve problems and support him.

The second quotation describes an experience of alienation. A mother who had been full of hope and excitement about her child's entry into kindergarten was frustrated and discouraged before the end of the first week of school. The kind of contact with the teacher that she experienced builds resentment, promotes conflict between family and school, and puts the child in the middle—and as in an acrimonious divorce, the child can't win. Considering that this is one of the first communications at the outset of this child's school career, it is hard to imagine how this mother and the teacher will work effectively and collaboratively to support the child if she indeed has some adjustment struggles in kindergarten.

This book's goal is to promote the kind of transition experiences reported by Nate's mother (and many other mothers, fathers, and children with whom we spoke) and to actively and systematically prevent the experience reported by the second mother. This volume draws on the experiences of parents, children, kindergarten teachers, principals, preschool teachers, and community agency staff to anchor these ideas and recommendations in reality. The primary goal is to facilitate positive, effective, stable relationships—among all of these groups of people—that serve to support children as they move into kindergarten and that build cohesion among many early education programs. Starting this process requires a model or framework for conceptualizing transition in order to guide transition planning.

THINKING ABOUT THE TRANSITION TO SCHOOL

The transition into kindergarten is an important time in children's lives, and it influences their later school careers. Children's early schooling can be considered a critical period that sets the trajectory for their future school adjustment (Belsky & MacKinnon, 1994; Pianta & Walsh, 1996). Experiencing early academic and social success can pave the way for children's later positive school adjustment. After the first several years of school, individual differences in academic performance are very stable (Alexander & Entwisle, 1988). A number of studies—including the National Institute of Child Health and Human Development (NICHD) Study of Early Child Care, the Abecedarian Study, and the High/Scope Perry Preschool Study—demonstrated that high-quality preschool and child care experiences enhance school success (see Pianta & Cox, 1999, for a summary).

Children face enormous discontinuities between preschool and kindergarten as they enter elementary school for the first time. These discontinuities, which also affect families and teachers, underscore the importance of this period. For example, as children enter elementary school after preschool, they and their families experience a substantial shift in culture and expectations, including more formal academic demands, a more complex social environment, less family support and connection, and less time with teachers due to larger class size and more transitions during the school day. This time period clearly warrants considerable attention.

When asked to discuss the transition process, parents identified several common themes (Kraft-Sayre & Pianta, 1999). Parents told us that they always anticipated school with excitement. They emphasized that good transition experiences do not come about solely through the school making contact and that contact with the school can both help and hurt, as noted by the two mothers quoted at the beginning of the chapter. Families also said they believe that transition planning and preparation by all involved need to start early. Most important, parents expressed a hope and desire that schools will get to know their children as individuals. These themes highlight the importance of ways in which relationships among the child, his or her family, and the school contribute to the transition process.

It is important to view transition not only from the perspective of families, preschool teachers, and children (i.e., the senders) but also from the perspective of elementary school teachers and administrators (i.e., the receivers). In a sense, transition is about communication, and the meaning and values that the senders and the receivers place on certain features of transition can affect whether and how transition planning creates smooth communication. One way to start asking the receivers about transition is to see whether kindergarten teachers have any concerns about children entering school. If kindergarten teachers were satisfied that nearly all children enter school ready to learn or felt that they could effectively reach and teach the majority of children who enter their classrooms, then there would be no real need for transition planning. People could spend their time and energy elsewhere. When a national sample of kindergarten teachers was asked about how well they thought children were making the transition into school, they expressed a surprising level of concern and a pressing need for better transition planning (Rimm-Kaufmann et al., 1999). When these teachers were asked how well children navigate the move from preschool to kindergarten, on average they indicated that about half of children make the transition successfully, another third have some problems, and almost 20% of children entering kindergarten experience serious difficulties with transition that affect the children and the teachers. When asked what factors contributed most to children's difficulties, kindergarten teachers were concerned about skills such as following directions and cooperating, working independently or in a group, and getting along with teachers and peers. They did not cite lack of academic skills as the primary concern, although it was frequently noted. In many ways, kindergarten teachers were mostly concerned about children's social development and how children were able to cooperate in the educational process by being teachable.

Very clear evidence exists that teachers and parents routinely agree that discontinuities between preschool and kindergarten pose challenges for children (and parents and teachers). A key issue, then, is identifying the ways in which schools bridge these differences and offer support to children and families as they move into school. Again, the national survey of kindergarten teachers found that the most common transition practices involve contacting families *after* school starts. Letters, flyers, notes, and back-to-school nights are the most widespread forms of transition practices but are fairly generic and impersonal. Unfortunately, they often occur too late in the transition process to do much good. In short, the most common things that schools do during transition periods are not what parents think would be beneficial to them and their children. Thus, the challenges experienced by children are not addressed by the most common ways schools try to help them. This disconnect between schools' and families' needs is most often a function of the model schools use to guide their transition practices. The least common transition practices involve visits or telephone calls to the child or the family, either before or after school starts.

MODELS OF TRANSITION

Children's transition into kindergarten can be considered in a variety of ways. To understand the approach to transition described in this volume, it is useful to describe other models of transition. Four ways to think about transition are 1) a *skills only model* that targets children's skills as the key influence on school adjustment, 2) an *environmental input model,* in which children's skills at any given time are influenced by their experiences in key settings, 3) a *linked environments model* that, building on the others, recognizes the importance of connections across settings (e.g., relationships between parents and preschool providers), and 4) a *developmental model* of transition, which incorporates all of the elements of the prior models, emphasizes connections and linkages across settings over time, and also informs our approach. (See Rimm-Kauffman & Pianta, 2001, for a fuller discussion of these models.)

The following presentation of the models of transition is not an academic exercise removed from the reality of practices and experiences—it is a useful tool that reflects them. The description of each model presents quotations from interviews we conducted with parents, teachers, school administrators, and other professionals connected with transition planning. The quotations offer a glimpse into the ways that these different people experience transition and the ideas that guide their work.

Skills Only Model

The *skills only model* is a child-focused perspective that views the transition to kindergarten in terms of the abilities and skills the child brings with him or her on the first day of school (see Figure 1.1). School adjustment is understood in terms of child characteristics, such as readiness and level of maturation.

"You start seeing behavior problems and adjustment problems in preschool. Sometimes at the start of kindergarten, it can still be just a maturity issue, but if it is a maturity issue, then at the end of kindergarten and the beginning of first grade they get over it."

Furthermore, in this model, children's problems in school may not be viewed as related to their transition experiences. Transition, in this case, is narrowly defined:

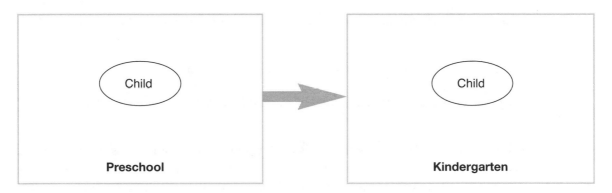

Figure 1.1.   The skills only model of transition. This model focuses only on the skills that the child has.

"This child doesn't have any problems with transition even though she has other issues, academic issues that I see, but not transition issues."

Although children's skills and abilities do indeed play a role in their adjustment to school (Alexander & Entwisle, 1988; Christian, Morrison, & Bryant, 1998), their skills and abilities do not account for the majority of individual differences in children's school adjustment (LaParo & Pianta, 1998; Pianta & McCoy, 1997). For example, measures of children's academic and cognitive abilities and skills in preschool account for less than 30% of the differences in these skills among children once they enter kindergarten. Measurements of the social skills valued by kindergarten teachers as signs of adjustment correspond even less in preschool and kindergarten. Thus, understanding transition outcomes requires focusing on influences on school outcomes beyond characteristics of the child.

Environmental Input Model

The *environmental input model* describes experiences in a variety of social settings as contributing to children's skills and adjustment at any given time (see Figure 1.2). Input from experiences with family, peers, school, and community settings affect the child's skills. For example, peer relationships and classroom characteristics, such as class size and classroom quality, influence the child's performance (Graue, 1999; Howes, 1990; Ladd & Price, 1987). Many people who agree with this model of transition believe that social experiences outside of school (e.g., whether a parent reads to the child, teaches him or her letters, or shows the child how to tie a shoe) can affect how a child adjusts to school.

School adjustment is viewed as a function of the structure and emotional climate of the classroom. Positive teacher qualities, a clear structure, and older peers serving as buddies can help children's transition to the new environment:

"Having nurturing qualities in teachers is what really helps any kid get used to school as a first-time experience."

"Setting limits and having a routine for them are important."

"I try to keep my schedule exactly the same, and if I can do that for them, then they're fine."

What is missing from this model is an emphasis on experiences over time and how different settings are connected to one another. The teachers quoted here do not see transition and school adjustment as interrelated processes. For them, the adjustment to school pertains strictly to what happens in the kindergarten classroom and not to the child's family relationships or previous experiences. These teachers understand transition as occurring only within this setting, and they do not connect this context with other contexts, such as the home environment or preschool experiences. Nor are contexts viewed as interacting over time. For example, this teacher does not see parental factors as related to children's adjustment:

"I don't think the parent's expectations really have a lot to do with how well the kids [make the] transition. Those are just parent issues that they have sometimes coming from certain situations, but that doesn't really make a difference to me at least with how the kids do."

Linked Environments Model

The *linked environments model* includes the ways in which connections between key settings or people in key settings in the child's life (e.g., the parents' comfort and communication with the preschool teacher) can affect the child's adjustment. In the linked environments model, children's skills; experiences with family, peers, schools, and the community; and the connections among

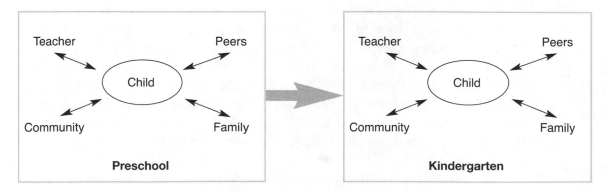

Figure 1.2.   The environmental input model of transition. This model recognizes the influences of the teacher, family, peers, and community.

and settings all influence school adjustment at a given time (see Figure 1.3). For example, family involvement indirectly influences children's school success. Strong connections between families and schools are linked with positive child outcomes beyond any direct effect the families or the schools have on children (Epstein, 1996; Reynolds, 1989). Although this model considers the interactions of multiple relationships surrounding the child, it regards these relationships as static rather than as developing over time.

Whereas some kindergarten teachers do not identify previous experiences and family background as contributing to children's school adjustment, others believe that positive family environments, preschool, and other structured experiences contribute to a successful transition. If children lack these experiences or face emotional challenges, teachers often feel that the adjustment to kindergarten may be a problem:

"Just the fact that they are in a preschool and doing something and not doing whatever they might do at home—at least they're being exposed to books one year earlier."

"I find the hardest children to deal with here in the classroom are those who are able to run free at home, who don't have the structure, and whose parents don't have control."

"The ones that have the biggest problems are the ones that haven't had a routine, and don't know what that is to have some expectations."

These teachers mention the importance of parent attitude and involvement in promoting children's adjustment. Parents' comfort level influences the transition for children:

"Parents' attitude plays a big part. If a parent doesn't want the child to come, it really plays on the child."

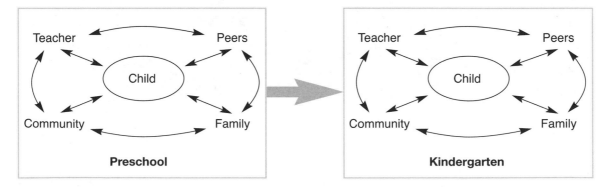

Figure 1.3. The linked environments model of transition. This model recognizes the influences of the teacher, family, peers, and community on each other, in addition to the child.

"The parents' perception of school, if they like school, if they are comfortable here, makes a big difference [to the child's transition]. They are just more at ease, and that goes back to their children and their children are more at ease here."

"Having the feeling that they're welcome at school and comfortable in the school and not intimidated and more willing to work together [are important]."

Developmental Model

The *developmental model* incorporates all of the components of these three perspectives and adds the important dimension of time, a critical aspect of the transition process. This model is described as developmental because it emphasizes change and development over time in the key features and experiences that affect children's adjustment to kindergarten. Child, family, school, peer, and community factors are interconnected and interdependent with one another not only at a given time but throughout the transition process (see Figure 1.4). Based on Bronfenbrenner and Morris's (1998) bioecological model and Pianta and Walsh's (1996) contextual systems model, the developmental model considers the key changes in relationships among the child, school, family, and community as the child moves from prekindergarten experiences to formal schooling. Rather than understanding a child's transition solely in terms of his or her skills or the influences on those skills at any given time, this perspective emphasizes how the connections and relationships that support the child develop over time.

When transition practices and plans foster positive relationships, they support the child's successful school adjustment. This model provides a framework for thinking about these relationships and generating ideas about which rela-

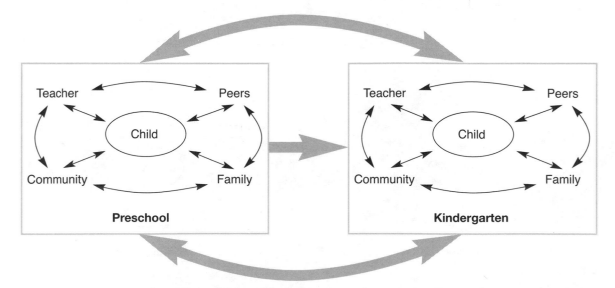

Figure 1.4. The developmental model of transition. This model recognizes the relationships among the child, teacher, family, peers, and community across time.

tionships to foster and how to develop them. Specifically, relationships between preschool teachers and kindergarten teachers, among peers, and between families and schools can serve as a bridge from preschool to kindergarten and foster children's adjustment. The developmental model of transition results in transition plans that help schools reach out to families before school starts, help communities foster links between preschools and kindergartens, and promote personal connections before the first day of school. In these ways, this model is consistent with the National Education Goals Panel's (1998) first goal that children will start school ready to learn and that schools will be ready for children.

The transition process is multifaceted and varies greatly from school to school. It depends on the perceptions of parents and teachers and their beliefs regarding the factors important to helping children adjust to kindergarten. Fundamentally, transition is a *process* that involves four facets: ready schools, community participation and support, family knowledge and involvement, and preschools and child care settings committed to preparing children. The goal of this transition approach is to facilitate an ongoing relationship-building process among all partners. In developing, designing, and implementing transition plans in communities and districts, we use a set of guiding principles to inform our work. These principles are derived from the way we think about transition and the available evidence of what makes a successful transition for children, families, and schools.

GUIDING PRINCIPLES

Five guiding principles form the core elements of transition planning and practices, and they can be applied to individual children, families, and schools in order to foster successful kindergarten transitions:

1. Foster relationships as resources

2. Promote continuity from preschool to kindergarten

3. Focus on family strengths

4. Tailor practices to individual needs

5. Form collaborative relationships

They are based on extensive analysis of recommended practices with young children and knowledge about supporting healthy child and family development. These principles guide the implementation of the transition practices described in this book. When used with the developmental model of transition, these principles help generate transition practices and policies and inform decisions about how to adjust or tailor practices to a given situation.

Foster Relationships as Resources

Supportive, effective relationships with children and with those who work and live with children are resources for child development. When a child is involved in and surrounded by supportive relationships, the transition to kindergarten occurs more smoothly. The importance of relationships as assets or resources is reflected in what this mother had to say about her connection to her child's school:

"I try to work with Julie's teacher and I tell her that anything I can do to help her as far as Julie's learning, to let me know. Because, I mean, we could definitely do it at home. Just by letting me know how she's doing and what I can do at home to help her. You know, just by talking to me."

Parents also benefit from positive relationships during the transition process, and teachers are a valued and useful source of support and information to parents, particularly first-time parents. During their child's move from preschool to kindergarten, some parents find that knowing the teacher already, perhaps from the community, can be helpful. The transition process for the parent quoted next was eased in part because she already knew her son's teacher, who had previously taught her older son.

"We have a close relationship. Marcus' older brother was in her class. We like each other a lot. I know if I have a problem, I'll usually write her and she'll always tell me something helpful. There have been times I've really needed that. Also, if she has a problem with Marcus, she knows she can get in touch with me. If there's been anything wrong, she asks me about it."

In these examples, each parent describes a relationship with the child's teacher that is helpful to her as a parent and that is indirectly helpful to her child. The child involved is supported through his or her relationship with the parent or teacher and through the positive relationship the parent and the teacher have with one another.

Promote Continuity from Preschool to Kindergarten

Relationships that are stable and lasting can serve as a bridge between the family and school and provide continuity from preschool to kindergarten. These relationships can be found among parents, teachers, family workers, other school staff, and the child's peers. For example, if preschools and kindergartens work together collaboratively, they are more likely to develop programs that are consistent and that build on one another. These relationships may be social in nature or may have an informational component or purpose. As one kindergarten teacher observed,

"I think some sort of consistency and structure probably really helps. That bridge between the two [preschool and school] would just be better if there were a lot of things we had in common. If the preschool would do some things that we do and if we did some things that [the] preschool did, then it would seem less like a totally different world. I think academics really help transitioning. I mean, if they did a lot of prereading kinds of activities over there [in preschool] and they built really strong foundations in that area, then I think when the kids get here, it's not so overwhelming. Because otherwise they get here and they don't know any of their numbers, they don't know any of their letters, and they don't know where they are, and they're twice as panicked. And if we know what they're doing, then I think that would help, too."

This kindergarten teacher described the need for an exchange of information between preschool and kindergarten, by which the expectations and experiences for children in preschool and kindergarten can be made more consistent and the discontinuities across the programs made less noticeable. Although this teacher has a particular view of what is important for preschool teachers to know and do (i.e., focus on academic skills), it is only through linking preschool and kindergarten teachers in a collaborative partnership and discussing these expectations and experiences that children's transitions can be supported more effectively. In providing consistency from year to year, programs offer developmentally sensitive transition practices that best support young children.

Focus on Family Strengths

Think about how the quotations at the beginning of this chapter suggest different ways that schools see families. In interactions with schools, how often do families feel blamed or viewed as the source of a child's problems? How often do schools feel ineffective in helping children? Too often the communication between families and schools reflects a combination of blaming and helplessness that goes both ways. Yet when we asked families and teachers about their experiences and looked at examples of successful family–school connections, we saw that it is clearly possible that relationships between schools and families, reflecting the *strengths* of families, can be developed through supportive, positive interactions initiated by the school. Approaching families as resources with special strengths, no matter how these are defined or

---

A Word About Readiness

How does readiness for kindergarten intersect with the way we think about transition? This is a very important question, in part because almost all of teachers' attention is focused on this issue of readiness, particularly the child's readiness to learn academic and social skills. We believe that readiness is an important and integral component of transition—it is in the center of our model! Any approach to fostering connections between parents and teachers should not be viewed as an end in itself but should be designed with the goal of helping a child function more effectively in a classroom. So school readiness is neither an overlay nor a subtext. It is very important, though, to note the different definitions of school readiness and the way it is valued. School and community leaders may see the issue of readiness from different perspectives while parents (or even the children) may view it from another. Furthermore, it is very likely that there are multiple definitions of readiness in any given community, each of which can be activated at any given time or situation. In some school districts, age becomes the means by which a district decides when a child is ready (even though the district may give extensive readiness screenings), yet parents are more interested in maturity and teachers are concerned about emergent literacy and children's ability to cooperate.

Typically, *readiness* is described as a set of skills, generally academic, the acquisition of which determines how successful a child is expected to be in kindergarten. Rather than viewing readiness as a static state that describes the child, the developmental model of transition incorporates readiness as a property of the *system* of families, schools, and programs that develops the desired competencies in children as they enter school. Thus, readiness incorporates the child's experiences at home, his or her experiences in preschool, the community resources that support high-quality child care and parenting practices, the elementary school's ability to incorporate these family and school resources, and the ability of kindergarten programs to build on a child's skills and competencies (Love, Aber, & Brooks-Gunn, 1992; Pianta & Walsh, 1996). Readiness is not simply a property of the child. It is a reflection of a preschool's preparation of a child, of a kindergarten's preparedness to welcome that child, and of the parents' recognition of the differences between preschool and kindergarten and their ability to manage those differences. All the personnel involved are responsible for working with each of the other components of the system to identify the skills and competencies that will enable a child to be ready for kindergarten and to identify what the school needs in order to be ready for the child and his or her family. Therefore, we highlight this definition by Pianta and Walsh, which stipulates that:

> Children are ready for school when, for a period of several years, they have been exposed to consistent stable adults who are emotionally invested in them; to a physical environment that is safe and predictable; to regular routines and rhythms of activity; to competent peers; and to materials that stimulate their exploration and enjoyment of the object world and from which they derive a sense of mastery. (1996, p. 34)

---

enacted, allows schools to build relationships that can be helpful to vulnerable children and families.

Families feel encouraged when their interactions with schools are based on their competencies, rather than on their failures. One single mother of four children works days and cannot come to meetings at the school. Her child is having problems learning to read and paying attention:

"It makes me feel good to see her [the school social worker]. She listens to me and doesn't make me feel bad for not coming to conferences or PTO [the parent–teacher organization].

She helped me and James' teacher put together a plan for his behavior and gave me some stuff to do at home with him for his reading. Things seem better now."

Tailor Practices to Individual Needs

The actual set of transition practices enacted with a given family or classroom must be based on the needs and strengths of that child, family, teacher, school, and community. This approach is menu-driven—it does not prescribe a list of things to do but instead suggests a number of alternatives that are based on the guiding principles. The approach is designed to be flexibly applied across a wide range of needs and strengths. When a rigid transition program is in place, certain needs are likely to be neglected and some efforts may be wasted, addressing needs that are not there.

"I'm satisfied that his teacher has his best interest at heart. I'm comfortable with [the teacher]. She doesn't lump him in with everybody else. She seems to look at him as an individual. She does seem to focus on his strong points. I don't know, she just makes us feel like she can see the real Matt. When I talk to her, she knows his weaknesses, she knows his strong points, and she asks me about him personally so she gets to know him better. So that's something that's gone really well."

Form Collaborative Relationships

Collaboration among the key players in the transition process—teachers, principals, family workers, families—is fundamental in developing and implementing successful transition practices. Throughout this book, we emphasize that these partnerships are very valuable and that good transition planning and practices are the products of effective partnerships and relationships.

"[Transition goes well when] everybody is comfortable with the process and the children are very familiar with the classroom, with the teacher, with the school. The families feel very comfortable. The teacher feels like they know the children that are coming in, which gives them an element of comfort, and all this is through the activities that we did."

Good partnerships and good relationships are not free of conflicts or disagreements. Instead, they need a commitment to a process of communicating about disagreements and resolving them that reflects common values regarding the child and a common way of thinking about what is important. When key players in the transition process adopt a common way of thinking about transition, a common frame of reference within which to resolve disagreements is created. These guiding principles offer another way of establishing a common ground. But, clearly, much of what goes on in transition planning involves reconciling different views about children, different values regarding skills or experiences, and different definitions. Conflict, disagreements, and differences of opinion are part of the relationships, collaborations, and partnerships that need to be formed. True partners work to resolve differences and reconcile, and, in the end, resourceful transition planning is the result.

How can these guiding principles be enacted to inform transition planning? First and foremost, professionals should use these principles in analyzing their current and intended practices. To what extent does a particular transition practice foster relationships? Does it lead to a sense of continuity and stability for the child and family moving from preschool to kindergarten? Does a practice identify or foster family strengths, or like many assessment practices, does it focus on weaknesses and risk? Another set of questions to pose addresses the context of practices. Are the same practices implemented for every family or do professionals tailor these efforts? Furthermore, do professionals work together to form their own collaborative relationships, or are transition practices solely the responsibility or initiative of one group?

SUMMARIZING THEMES

A developmental model of kindergarten transition considers child factors; the child's social network of family, school, peer, and community; and the interactions of these contexts over time. This model suggests facilitating the connections among children, families, schools, and communities to foster the transition process. A community transition plan should reflect common principles of fostering relationships; promoting continuity from preschool to kindergarten; focusing on family strengths; developing a menu-driven, flexible, and individually tailored array of practices; and engaging in a collaborative team process.

The next chapters describe how to put a developmental model of transition into action. We describe specific steps to take to ensure an effective, supportive transition process in your school and community.

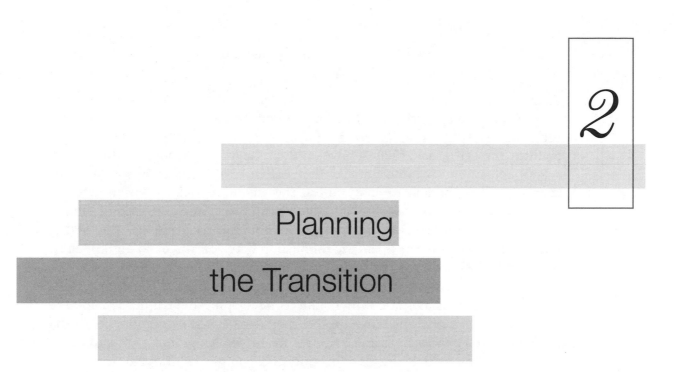

Planning
the Transition

"There's always a transition and anxiety when you go from one grade to another—different teacher, different groups of kids that you'll be with. So we always try to make the adjustment good all the way around."

"Most kids are really excited about coming to kindergarten even if it's the first day they've stepped into the building. I don't see a whole lot of problems with kindergarten transitioning. I don't see a whole lot of kids who are not happy."

Helping children and their families make the transition to kindergarten involves careful planning and consideration of an array of transition practices appropriate to the needs of the families, schools, and communities. A person's definition of the transition into kindergarten informs how he or she understands transition. Is transition viewed as a static event involving the action of a child entering the kindergarten classroom, or is transition a dynamic process involving many factors over time? Does transition play an important role in children's school adjustment, or is it considered a relatively inconsequential issue for children? If transition is an issue, to what are successes or problems in children's transition into school attributed? Is there a focus on the child, the child's family, the preschool or elementary school, or the relationships among these; or is some other contributing process involved?

The four models of transition, described in detail in Chapter 1, capture the different ways that school personnel conceptualize children's transitions into school. Although some similarities exist in all of the perspectives, preschool teachers, kindergarten teachers, principals, and family workers view the transition process in distinct ways. To briefly review, the skills only model is a child-focused perspective that views the transition to kindergarten in terms of the abilities and skills that children have on their first day of school. In this model, school adjustment is understood in terms of children's characteristics, such as their readiness and level of maturation. The second model, the environmental input model, acknowledges social contexts as contributing to school adjustment but does not consider the interaction among these contexts. The linking environments model considers the interaction between the child and the various systems with which the child interacts. The child, family, peers, schools, and community all influence school adjustment. However, this model regards these relationships as static rather than as developing over time. Finally, the developmental model of transition incorporates all of the components of the previous three perspectives and accounts for the development of relationships over time. This model regards transition as a complex and dynamic process. Multiple factors—child, family, school, peers, and community—are interconnected and interdependent with one another through the transition process.

This chapter describes a concrete approach to developing a transition plan in a community or school. The ideas and approach are based on extensive applications of this approach during a period of 5 years in a range of schools and communities. This approach has been adopted statewide in several states as a guide for facilitating transition in local communities and unifying the approach to early childhood programming for children from birth to age 8. It has also been used in large urban areas that have very high rates of child poverty and non–English-speaking families. Finally, it has been applied in dozens of smaller communities and individual schools as a way of facilitating transitions for children and families.

PLANNING AND IMPLEMENTATION

Although the change from preschool to kindergarten is inevitable for children, a successful and well-organized transition is not. Transition is not simply an event best represented by the first day of school, nor is it a procedure that can successfully occur by happenstance. Rather, the transition to kindergarten is a process that starts in preschool and continues through the early months of kindergarten. The change affects parents, teachers, and schools. In order for children, families, and schools to experience the most positive and productive transition from preschool to kindergarten, the needs, expectations, and goals of all of the participants should be considered. As highlighted in the guiding principles, forethought and planning enable families and schools to capitalize on the resources embodied in the relationships children have with their teachers, the relationships families and schools have with each other, and the strengths of individual families. In addition, designing transitions allows schools to promote continuity from preschool to kindergarten and to identify and respond to the individual needs of children, families, schools, and communities.

Levels of Planning and Implementation

Before discussing the specific steps to planning and implementation, it is important to recognize that these procedures and steps can take place at multiple levels within a community or region. This approach has been found useful at the state, city, town, and individual school levels. For the purposes of this book, we focus on the two most common levels—communities and individual schools within a community. Over the next several chapters, we describe nine steps to successful kindergarten transition. For many steps, we present specific tools for facilitating progress on particular steps. Figure 2.1 organizes these tools as they fit with specific steps.

Steps to Kindergarten Transition	
Step	**Helpful tool**
Step 1 Establish Collaborative Teams	
Step 2 Identify a Transition Coordinator	
Step 3 Facilitate Regular Meetings and Conduct a Needs Assessment	Transition Interview (Figure A1, p. 91)
Step 4 Generate Ideas for Transition Activities	Transition Practices Brainstorming Guide (Figure A2, p. 92)
Step 5 Create a Transition Timeline	Transition Timeline Worksheet (Figure A3, p. 93)
Step 6 Anticipate Barriers	
Step 7 Revise Ideas and Timelines	Checklist for Community Transition Steering Committees (Figure A4, p. 94)
Step 8 Implement Transition Practices	Checklist for Transition Coordinators (Figure A5, p. 94)
	Checklist for Preschool Teachers (Figure A6, p. 95)
	Checklist for Kindergarten Teachers (Figure A7, p. 95)
	Checklist for Principals (Figure A8, p. 95)
Step 9 Assess, Evaluate, and Revise	Kindergarten Transition Contact Log (Figure A9, p. 96)
	Kindergarten Transition Menu Checklist (Figures A10–A11, pp. 97–98)
	Kindergarten Transition Parent Interviews (Figures A12–A13, pp. 99–105)
	Transition Activities Questionnaires (Figures A14–A19, pp. 106–116)
	Transition Interview (Figure A1, p. 91)

Figure 2.1. Steps and helpful tools for successful kindergarten transition.

Community Planning   Much of transition planning requires work at the community level. For many communities, the community level and school system level are synonymous. Community-level work is important in transition planning for two reasons. First, leaders at the community level (e.g., superintendents, city council members, agency directors) control the allocation of resources and policy making that can put transition planning on the agendas of the necessary groups; can make transition planning a priority of these groups; and can direct resources, attention, and organization in ways that facilitate the development of effective transition practices for children and families. These leaders also set policy that has a large effect on transition planning (e.g., the date and location of kindergarten registration).

The second way in which communities are involved with transition planning involves community-level linkages that reflect transition practices, through which families encounter various aspects of the wider community in ways that foster good transitions. For example, when a community uses its wider home-based agencies and outreach resources to help parents provide literacy opportunities for children that are consonant with and developed by the school system, then community-level contacts support transition. When a community mobilizes to publicize kindergarten registration and a variety of volunteers and agency workers who are in contact with families help those families register their children (which enables these families in turn to be contacted by their child's kindergarten teacher long before school starts), then community-level contacts are supporting transition.

Developing a community transition plan involves the following steps, each of which are essential to smooth implementation of transition practices. Each step needs to be enacted at the district or community level, as well as at the level of individual schools, programs, or neighborhoods, as portrayed in Figure 2.2. As the model depicts, effective transition programs are organized on two different levels. At the community level, a Community Transition Steering Committee, an interdisciplinary, collaborative team, is formed that designs, coordinates, and evaluates transition programs for the school district. This team serves as the steering committee for transition programs that are implemented at the school level, providing continuity across programs while allowing schools to address their unique needs through school-level teams.

School-Level Planning   School Transition Teams focus on the needs and resources specific to their program and families and design the strategies that maximize the impact of the community-based transition program for their school population. For example, they take into account the number of children to be served, the locations of the preschool programs relative to the elementary school, and the diversity of families within their school catchment area. Difficulties, needs, and successes should be discussed at the community level, so that each school benefits and learns from the experiences of the other participating programs.

Roles, Responsibilities, and Goals

Figure 2.2 notes who takes part in these two levels of transition partnerships. A variety of key personnel are involved, although the people listed may vary from community to community or across schools within a community. In one school, a lead kindergarten teacher may serve as the transition coordinator, while in another school in the same system, the teacher in the prekindergarten program may serve in the same role.

Community Transition Steering Committees   The Community Transition Steering Committee in a given school system or community has several crucial roles, responsibilities, and goals:

- Identify community-wide transition needs for parents, children, schools, and preschools

- Identify current transition practices and resources in the community

- Provide resources and direction for development of local transition teams in each school catchment

- Provide support for the development of transition policies and practices

- Provide for coordination and organization across various agencies and constituencies

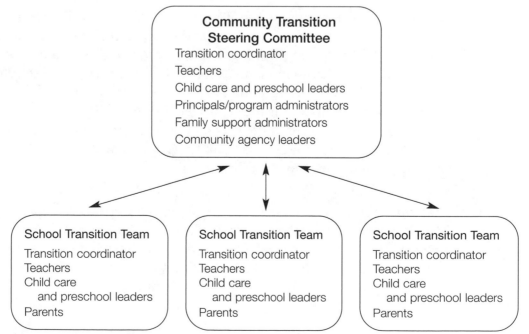

Figure 2.2.   Community-level and school-level transition teams work together.

- Develop transition planning as a priority in the community and in local settings

- Identify a community-wide leader or spokesperson related to transition issues

Local School-Level Transition Teams   The School Transition Team in a local school building or school catchment area has a different set of roles, responsibilities, and goals:

- Identify key personnel related to transition in that school

- Meet regularly

- Identify transition needs for parents, children, and teachers in that school and in preschools serving that school

- Identify current transition practices and resources in the school

- Develop a transition plan and associated transition practices in that school

- Identify a transition coordinator for that school

- Implement, evaluate, and revise transition on an ongoing basis

STEP 1   ESTABLISH COLLABORATIVE TEAMS

Establishing collaborative teams of preschool teachers, kindergarten teachers, family workers, principals, parents, and other representatives at community and school levels is critical in planning, implementing, and evaluating a community's kindergarten transition plan. This group should include those who will be affected directly by the transition of preschoolers into kindergarten (i.e., teachers, parents, and school principals), as well as those who are indirectly affected but have a vested interest in the program's success (e.g., district administrators, community representatives). One family worker describes the frustration that can occur when teams do not collaborate:

"[The transition program] wasn't understood by the school. It was something that I, being the family worker, took on and talked to the teacher about. Not that it would ever happen because of their time schedules, but the teachers, there wasn't that kind of connection there. [There] wasn't an understanding of exactly why it was occurring. I don't even think it was even on the administrative side, really."

The community's transition steering committee should be selected from leaders (or their designees) at the community level (e.g., superintendents, city council members, agency directors). It is important that these members control allocation of resources and policy making that can put transition planning on the agenda of the necessary groups; make transition planning a priority of these groups; and direct resources, attention, and organization in order to facilitate the development of effective transition practices for children and families. These leaders set policy that significantly affects transition planning. Initially, the community or school system leadership must make a commitment to better transition planning and programs. This process can have many origins: staff, families, or interested others. The critical feature of this phase of planning is that at the community or district level, leaders are designated to participate on this level's transition planning team. Most of the time, the process involves inviting participation from agencies or school administration and taking volunteers. At the community or district level, the transition steering committee typically involves a number of relevant agencies in that location (e.g., health agencies, child care services, schools, library services, early education/ Head Start programs, parent groups).

At the school level, a similar team should be formed, composed of parents, preschool and kindergarten teachers, school administrators, and community members. This school-level transition steering team is responsible for adapting the district's plan to the unique needs of individual programs. The school-level teams typically involve kindergarten teachers, the principal, a school social worker or Title I program coordinator, a special education teacher, parents, child care agencies in the school's catchment, and sometimes a health services agency. It is a good idea to limit this group to no more than eight members and to make sure there are as many or more nonschool members as elementary school members.

STEP 2 | IDENTIFY A TRANSITION COORDINATOR

At the community level, a transition coordinator should be identified to serve organizational and supportive functions and help the school transition coordinators implement the programs, identify resources, and address any difficulties unique to the individual schools. The function of the transition coordinator can be filled by an agency leader, guidance counselor, principal, program coordinator, or other school administrator who incorporates this role into their current duties. The primary responsibility of the transition coordinator is that of facilitator.

At the school level, a member of the school community who can serve as a bridge for families from the preschool to the kindergarten should be chosen. This individual might be a family worker, parent coordinator, preschool or kindergarten teacher, guidance counselor, or school social worker. (School systems may vary in terms of both the titles and functions of these positions.) The key is to designate someone to provide continuity and to coordinate transition activities in each school or program. This person should be familiar with the needs of children in both preschool and kindergarten, have ready knowledge of the needs of families and schools, and be able to identify resources available to support the transition plan. In one implementation of this approach, a preschool program's social worker served in this capacity. In another regional application, the Title I coordinator for a small school district served this role. The transition coordinator in another school system was the lead public health nurse. The important points about the role of transition coordinator are that the person filling this role should be good at communicating with diverse families and knowledgeable about the elementary school, preschools, and community services in which children are involved. Leadership and organizational skills are assets.

STEP 3 | FACILITATE REGULAR MEETINGS AND CONDUCT A NEEDS ASSESSMENT

The team coordinator (at the community or school level) also arranges for regular team meetings and facilitates discussions. At these meetings, the various perspectives and priorities of the programs, schools, and families involved are considered and incorporated into the transition plan. A community partnership involving the key participants can promote a cooperative process in which a realistic transition plan can be developed and implemented. This cooperation is essential so that all participants understand the purpose, goals, and plan for the transition process. The continuity and collaboration that best support students cannot be obtained otherwise.

A crucial part of this process is forming collaborative partnerships and common definitions of transition among people who often have differing views. Participants are likely to have different priorities and areas of emphasis in identifying the factors related to transition. Four members of the same team were interviewed, and a look at what they had to say reflects each member's unique perspective. One preschool teacher described children's needs in this way:

"Children need to feel good about themselves and their accomplishments. Their self-esteem is critical. I don't think it's as important that they know every letter, upper and lowercase, and can rattle off all these numbers and do beautiful representational pictures. I don't think that's what makes the child [feel good]. To be able to follow routine, to be able to listen to what someone else is saying, and to be able to use their words to express their feelings are critical to their success more than the academics of school—being able to hang up a backpack, flush a toilet. That's important because if you can't do those things and you're constantly tugging on your kindergarten teacher, then you get labeled as this needy, bad kid and then that whole process snowballs."

The school principal on that team emphasized how transition is facilitated by families' work with children:

"I would have to say that students who have had experiences with reading, going to libraries, [and] playing with more educational things and whose parents interact with them all the time and use everything as a teachable moment certainly do better. It's those students who come to us who have never been read to, who have never had any exposure at all to print or to anything like that who are having the most difficult time."

In the same meeting, a parent emphasized the need for the school to contact parents early:

"The orientation that the school gives, the spring orientation that they give when the preschools come in to visit, and then the school orientation—the conferences are pretty late, 2 months later, but I think they're good. I think that way the teacher can tell you exactly where your child is and what they need to work on, stuff like that."

And finally, the kindergarten teacher focused on parents' roles in making the transition hard or easy for children.

"Where I see difficulty with transition is with the parents. In preschool, there tends to be a lot more parent contact, and in kindergarten that separation from being so directly involved is beginning."

Clearly, everyone has different viewpoints, and part of the initial and ongoing planning of transition practices is to allow those viewpoints to be expressed and melded into a common perspective. One of the direct benefits of the developmental model of transition is that it is so comprehensive that it can incorporate a wide variety of viewpoints, and each team member can feel that his or her view is being valued.

Community Transition Steering Committees and School Transition Teams should discuss several topics, such as

- Educational and social issues affecting the school district, including the diversity of the children and families, financial resources and limitations, special needs populations, and the impact of poverty on the community

- The meaning of *transition* for the children, families, schools, and the community and the meaning of *readiness* for the schools in this community

- The strengths and weaknesses of the district's current transition program. For example, what skills, competencies, behaviors, and attitudes are currently being transmitted from preschool to kindergarten? How are they related to the goals of the transition program? How prepared do kindergarten teachers believe preschoolers are when they arrive? What are the patterns of family involvement from preschool to kindergarten? Do parents think the current program meets their needs? What would help children make the transition more smoothly?

- The relationship between preschool and kindergarten programs. For example, what competencies are necessary for success in kindergarten? What skills do preschool teachers think are important for children to learn? What skills do kindergarten teachers expect children to have when they arrive?

The team coordinator must solicit perspectives from all members of the team and facilitate discussions that prioritize needs for the process as a whole. At the school level, similar meetings should be held that focus on the unique needs of individual programs.

During the initial needs assessment phase, each team member should be responsible for gathering information about transition needs in the school from their own expertise or experience. This process may take several weeks and involve several meetings. It may also require information the community agencies collect, such as the number of children expected to enroll in school in the next several years, characteristics of families, availability and use of child care and community resources, or other information.

During the needs assessment process, the team leader should use large poster paper to track input from various members and summarize the themes and information arising from the discussion. The Transition Interview is also helpful (see Appendix Figure A1). At some point, the team leader should write a brief report (two or three pages) summarizing the transition needs in that school and have the team approve it. This forms the basis for the next stage of planning.

STEP 4   GENERATE IDEAS FOR TRANSITION ACTIVITIES

Once the needs of the schools and the community have been identified and the goals for transition set, each transition team should generate a working list, or *menu*, of transition-related activities and programs. This list of ideas is important because it allows programs, schools, and teachers to individualize and choose the intervention practices that are most useful to them and the families they serve. In particular, committees should take care to ensure that the interventions are aimed at addressing the needs outlined during their meetings. Activities also should aim to increase the number and intensity of the connections among the different partners in the transition program as described by the developmental model. That is, your team should try to identify ways to address the need for family–school, child–school, peer, and community connections. Most of the things a school is already doing to promote transition should remain on the list; however, it is important that the team try to generate additional ideas.

In the process of generating ideas for transition practices, teams and team members may find it helpful to refer to the developmental model and the five guiding principles for transition planning (Figure 2.3).

Here are the steps for generating ideas:

1. Using the model and the guiding principles and following the procedures of good brainstorming (in which ideas are allowed and freely expressed without critical comments), generate a working list of ideas for transition activities. Identify whether these are social connections (e.g., teachers calling parents) or informational connections (e.g., preschool teachers meeting with kindergarten teachers to smooth the curriculum and expectations). It may be helpful to use the Transition Practices Brainstorming Guide. An example form is available in the Appendix (Figure A2).

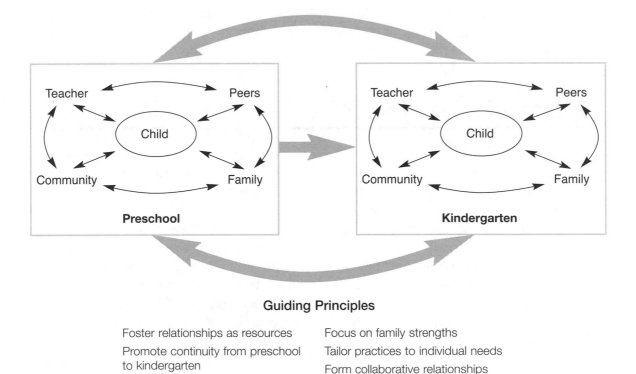

Guiding Principles

Foster relationships as resources   Focus on family strengths

Promote continuity from preschool   Tailor practices to individual needs
to kindergarten   Form collaborative relationships

Figure 2.3.   The developmental model of transition and its guiding principles.

2. Once a working list has been generated, identify the common links or inter-dependencies among the transition practices identified. Try to see ways in which different practices are or could be linked with one another (e.g., register children for kindergarten in April, assign children to class lists in May, invite children and families to meet their kindergarten teacher in June, hold school playground nights and have teachers call children and parents during the summer).

3. Prioritize the transition practices. Discuss each practice in terms of how important it is, the need that it fulfills, how easy it will be to implement, and the ways in which this practice may be packaged with other practices.

4. Identify the people involved in implementing the practices listed.

The resulting set of prioritized and discussed transition practices is the Transition Practices Brainstorming Guide—the first draft of your Transition Practices Menu, which you will use in Step 8 (see Chapter 3). This draft serves as a tool in selecting transition strategies and as a springboard for ideas for additional practices. Ongoing and regular meetings of the collaborators at various levels are necessary to ensure smooth and timely implementation. Using the completed Transition Practices Brainstorming Guide, your team can now proceed to Step 5, which is the creation of a Transition Timeline.

STEP 5 | CREATE A TRANSITION TIMELINE

A Transition Timeline outlines the plan for implementing the practices listed in the Transition Practices Brainstorming Guide developed in Step 4. The Transition Timeline Worksheet can assist you in mapping out transition strategies. To create a Transition Timeline, teams should take the guide completed in Step 4 and transpose the prioritized practices onto the Transition Timeline Worksheet. Make sure that transition practices are described in concrete terms and that they are placed on the Transition Timeline Worksheet for a specific date (and place when possible). You can find a Transition Timeline Worksheet in Appendix Figure A3. Note that some practices carry over from month to month (e.g., team meetings, sending home learning activities). These can be noted as well. However, the time invested now will pay off later.

Successful transition programs take a considerable amount of planning. For each group of entering preschoolers, the transition team should already have a transition plan in place. Consequently, the team should plan the program 1 year in advance of needing it. When surveying the sample timeline provided, keep in mind that although the process for each year's new kindergartners (i.e., from preschool fall through kindergarten fall) is represented as if each group of children entered in isolation, in actuality the strategies for preschool and kindergarten are implemented simultaneously each fall, as last year's preschoolers are now this year's kindergartners. Thus, Transition Timelines for different groups of children and families overlap from year to year as two different sets of children are being served.

The Community Transition Steering Committee creates a timeline for the overall transition plan across schools and programs. Critical in this timeline is the implementation of transition activities *prior* to the onset of kindergarten. Although some transition practices occur after the beginning of the school year, most of the transition activities need to be offered *before* kindergarten begins and require extensive planning. Timing is an important consideration for families. Parents appreciate having adequate preparation time and being able to start the transition process early. One parent responded very positively to the timing of her school district's transition practices:

"Right after the new year last year and [in] January or February, we started talking about kindergarten. So it gave us several months to think about all the paperwork and the details that we needed to get done. And it was brought up so early that [the plan] was there for the children. It wasn't so overwhelming, like when you wait until the last minute and all of a sudden, boom—you're going to kindergarten. It was early in the year and it was sort of slow. I don't think you could have done it any better with all the activities and bringing all the paperwork right to us in a package. And you fed us and gave us books at the same time. I don't think there's anything that could have been done that would have made the transition any easier."

Remember that strengthening the linkages between children and their families with schools before the start of school can ease families' concerns and ward off problems down the road. If problems do arise, the established pattern of positive interaction may help resolve them more easily and promptly. Knowing the teacher, the school secretary, and the principal can ease parents' minds. The transition process is enhanced when this relationship is established, and parents believe that teachers are sensitive to their children's needs, as indicated by these mothers.

"If I have a problem, I call the school, I know the secretary, she knows me, and I know the principal very well."

"Oh, goodness. I love that he's there. He's doing great. The teacher says so many nice things about him. And [the principal] knows me through [his brother] and he [said], 'I know you. You've got a five-year-old.' So, that make me feel nice when they recognize who you are."

In addition, when a family's initial school contact is a meeting with the teacher before the start of kindergarten to learn about the classroom and share information about their child, a positive tone is set for future interactions. Should a concern arise later in the school year, parents and teachers can rely on the groundwork for effective communication that has already been laid. When the parents have previously shared information with the teacher about their child's particular needs, they are more likely to feel that the teacher has a greater understanding of their situation. If a family's first contact with their child's teacher is a parent conference to discuss their child's behavior problems in the classroom, however, an entirely different relationship with the school is created and future interactions are more likely to be negative. Opportunities for positive family–school interaction are an integral part of the transition process.

With a focus on starting transition activities during the preschool year regardless of whether the child is enrolled in formal preschool services, the Transition Timeline Worksheet is a tool for the transition team to use to implement opportunities for social and informational connections from preschool through the transition into kindergarten. Families, children, and teachers should be involved in school and the transition process from as early as the fall of the preschool year. Practices that are most obviously related to transition (e.g., school visits) can be added in the spring of preschool. Emphasis on promoting peer relationships outside of school should increase over the course of preschool and through the summer before kindergarten. The late summer through the beginning of kindergarten is an ideal time for schools to offer more traditional transition activities (e.g., open houses, back-to-school nights). The timeline in Figure 2.4 provides an example of how this process might occur.

Preschool ⟶		Summer ⟶		Kindergarten
September	April	June	August	September
• Build family–school relationships • Conduct family group meetings • Foster peer relationships • Promote family participation	• Have preschool and kindergarten teachers coordinate efforts • Determine class lists for kindergarten • Invite preschoolers and their families to visit the kindergarten • Promote peer relationships outside of school	• Conduct summer programs • Provide home literacy activities • Offer school playground nights • Address family transition concerns	• Offer open houses • Have kindergarten teachers and parents meet • Conduct kindergarten screenings	• Offer back-to-school nights • Have the transition coordinator foster connections between families and kindergarten teachers

Figure 2.4.   A sample transition timeline for enhancing kindergarten transition.

Once a Transition Timeline Worksheet is drafted with the practices from the previously developed Transition Practices Brainstorming Guide, your team should also identify any planning, resources, or "behind the scenes" efforts needed to prepare for implementing a given activity. These actions should then be placed on the Transition Timeline Worksheet as well in order to denote their importance and role in the overall transition plan.

At the school level, school transition teams must specify a more detailed timeline for implementing the transition plan within their school community, taking into account their own needs, resources, and limitations. In addition, timelines could be created for each member of the team, so that roles and responsibilities are clearly defined. Sample timelines for the transition coordinator, kindergarten teacher, and preschool teacher are shown in Figures 2.5, 2.6, and 2.7.

STEP 6   ANTICIPATE BARRIERS

By the time you reach Step 6, you are almost halfway there! But before you can begin to implement your transition plan, it is important to consider the factors that might discourage or prevent members of the team from actively participating in and supporting the transition. The team must examine potential limitations on school resources, including finances, personnel, and time. For example, some districts do not have additional funds to pay personnel for extra work in the summer. Other districts do not have transportation available in the summer, and some resist the reallocation of personnel to the role of transition coordinator. In addition, factors that may potentially bar parents from being active participants in the transition process should be identified early so that ways around these barriers can be included in the transition plan.

Going back to the Transition Practices Brainstorming Guide and the Transition Timeline Worksheet that you developed, your team should now discuss any barriers related to the practices or events listed. A number of barriers exist for parents that prevent them from being as involved in their child's schooling as they would like to be. Work schedules are the predominant impediment to parents and affect involvement in both preschool and kindergarten. Parents working a day shift experience difficulty attending daytime meetings and school functions and sometimes lack the energy to attend meetings before or after school and work. Parents working evenings or night shifts have difficulty attending after-school events. Many parents feel frustrated by their inability to participate:

"I wish I could do more of the trips with the students and stuff but I can't because I have to work every day. Like they're going to the zoo. I wish I could go but I can't."

Preschool fall → **Preschool spring** → **Summer** → **Kindergarten fall**

Preschool fall	Preschool spring	Summer	Kindergarten fall
• Make contact with families, especially during the first 2 weeks of school • Assess family needs and refer for services if necessary • Encourage family participation • Offer newsletters or other resource materials • Establish peer connections • Foster inter-school collaboration about programs and classroom practices • Identify and communicate community expectations regarding curriculum • Initiate regular meetings at the school with families once per month • Meet regularly with the transition team	• Conduct practices from the fall • Work with school administrators to generate class lists • Encourage peer connections outside of school • Introduce children to their kindergarten teachers • Visit the elementary school • Establish connections with non-classmate peers who will be in the same kindergarten class • Help initiate preschool–elementary school connections around special events • Help initiate meetings between preschool and kindergarten teachers about students	• Continue practices from the fall and spring • Encourage kindergarten teachers to make contact with families • Encourage home-learning activities • Help coordinate information sharing between schools	• Continue practices from the fall, spring, and summer • Coordinate groups based on peer connections • Encourage the preschool teacher to contact former students • Help organize orientation for parents

Figure 2.5.   A sample transition timeline for transition coordinators.

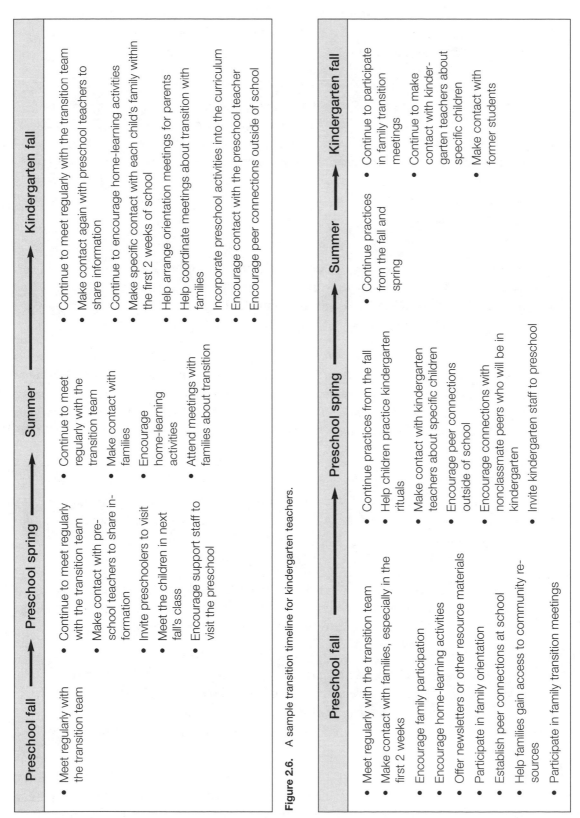

Preschool fall →	Preschool spring →	Summer →	Kindergarten fall
• Meet regularly with the transition team	• Continue to meet regularly with the transition team • Make contact with pre-school teachers to share information • Invite preschoolers to visit • Meet the children in next fall's class • Encourage support staff to visit the preschool	• Continue to meet regularly with the transition team • Make contact with families • Encourage home-learning activities • Attend meetings with families about transition	• Continue to meet regularly with the transition team • Make contact again with preschool teachers to share information • Continue to encourage home-learning activities • Make specific contact with each child's family within the first 2 weeks of school • Help arrange orientation meetings for parents • Help coordinate meetings about transition with families • Incorporate preschool activities into the curriculum • Encourage contact with the preschool teacher • Encourage peer connections outside of school

Figure 2.6. A sample transition timeline for kindergarten teachers.

Preschool fall →	Preschool spring →	Summer →	Kindergarten fall
• Meet regularly with the transition team • Make contact with families, especially in the first 2 weeks • Encourage family participation • Encourage home-learning activities • Offer newsletters or other resource materials • Participate in family orientation • Establish peer connections at school • Help families gain access to community resources • Participate in family transition meetings	• Continue practices from the fall • Help children practice kindergarten rituals • Make contact with kindergarten teachers about specific children • Encourage peer connections outside of school • Encourage connections with nonclassmate peers who will be in kindergarten • Invite kindergarten staff to preschool	• Continue practices from the fall and spring	• Continue to participate in family transition meetings • Continue to make contact with kindergarten teachers about specific children • Make contact with former students

Figure 2.7. A sample transition timeline for preschool teachers.

"I haven't been able to get into the meeting part, like when they have a family social kind of thing. I feel, though, you work all day and then you have to go to a meeting all night long and I know I should at least try to help out but it's hard."

"Actually, this year, I haven't been [as] involved as I wanted to be or as I was last year. I was more involved last year. I'm thinking part of that could be because of my personal situation. My job not being a straight job and not having the time to take off like I want to, to go to school. Last year, I came to a lot of programs and stuff that they had. This year, I haven't had any. This year, I didn't have much time to go over to the school at all, sit in the classroom. I mean, I've participated in some of the evening stuff like that but not some of the other stuff. I haven't made it to a PTO [meeting]. I feel bad. They got one coming up. [I'll] try to make it to that."

Some parents try to stay involved by sending in supplies for special school projects when their work schedule prevents them from attending functions. They are interested in being involved in whatever way they can be:

"I try to be involved. I probably did a little bit more last year because I had more [time] job wise. I would like to go in and do a little bit more, but I went on field trips with [my child] many times. I'll at least try to do it once or twice this school year to either go on a field trip or come in and be there. Like Halloween, I made cupcakes, so I try to be involved. I may have been more involved last year when she was in [preschool] than this year."

"I try to help out in the classes when they need extra parents there. I've been trying, but my job, I can't like go on the field trips and stuff like that but I can send in stuff and help out, whenever I can around there. Last year was easy. I could do stuff like that, but this year I can't do that much."

Some parents challenged by work or their school demands struggle to participate as much as possible. If they are unable to attend formal school functions, they try, at a minimum, to attend parent–teacher conferences.

"I have a heavy load at school because I'm graduating this summer—but it hasn't been much. I think it will be much more once I finish this semester. I'll finish early enough so that I can be involved. But not as much. I haven't been to any—well, I did go to the book fair—I've been really just trying to get over, set, and settled. But conferences, I've been to. I've been involved in that."

The ongoing stresses of life, such as illness and transportation problems, also make visiting the school difficult. Some parents find that they can still be involved by calling or corresponding with the teacher by notes, as well as by sending in items for classroom projects.

"I really haven't been able to get into a conference yet. It seems like I'm always missing them because of one of the kids being sick or something else going on that I can't get there. The car's broken down. But, other than that, I call [to find out] what's going on and if I get a letter home, [my child's] not doing right, I call to find out what I can do about it."

"Well, I haven't really been over to the school. I went to the conference and the meetings and stuff like that but as far as trying to donate my time or participating in anything—See, I got sick right at the beginning. Whatever they ask me to send, I'll do that, I'll donate items."

Some parents do not participate because they are uncomfortable in groups of people. Opportunities for involvement need to be tailored for these parents to give them an opportunity to interact with the teacher on a one-to-one basis.

"I don't get involved. I'm just not a people person. I mean, when I talk to people, I get along with them fine, but I don't like big crowds. When I was younger, it was a little different because I was a kid then. But now that I'm older, it's harder for me to talk to people."

Parents clearly have a variety of reasons for not getting involved in their children's schooling. When we asked parents about barriers, they described a range of problems, as shown in Table 2.1. (A group of 110 parents reported.) Consideration of these factors during the planning process may enable the transition committees, at both the school and district levels, to identify creative solutions that encourage more involvement. It may also help to ask some parents who are involved in their children's schooling about what enables them to participate.

The difficulties for teachers participating in transition programs should also be considered by the transition committees. In our sample of teachers, an

Table 2.1. Parents' barriers to participation in transition activities

Barrier	Percentage of parents reporting the barrier
Have a work schedule that interferes	74
Choose not to participate	17
Need child care	17
Lack transportation	16
Have a school schedule that interferes	14
Do not know others at school	14
Feel uncomfortable at school	9
Have health problems	9

Table 2.2 Teachers' barriers to participation in transition activities

Barrier	Percentage of teachers reporting the barrier
Activity requires work in summer that is not supported by salary	43
Class lists were generated too late	38
Parents are not interested or able to participate	30
Activity takes too much time	22
Transition practices plan is not available in the school/district	16
Funds are not available	14
Most parents who need the activity cannot be reached	14
Concerned about creating negative expectations	8
Visiting students' homes is dangerous	8
Choose not to do it	8
Contact with parents prior to the start of school is discouraged	3

assortment of barriers were identified (see Table 2.2). Many important and valuable transition activities would ideally be conducted in the evening or during the summer. Having activities during these times infringes on teachers' vacation and nonsalaried time. When asked about barriers to their participation in transition activities, kindergarten teachers identified this lack of pay as an important consideration as to whether they participated. The team may need to consider alternate ways of funding teachers for this involvement or providing incentives to encourage participation in order to maximize the involvement of teachers during the transition process. At the end of your discussion of barriers, try to identify ways in which your team can address these barriers and note them on the brainstorming guide.

STEP 7　REVISE IDEAS AND TIMELINES

Once the barriers have been identified, committees at both the school and the district levels need to revise their ideas and timelines to accommodate the identified barriers. There should be an ongoing loop through Steps 4–7, generating ideas and timelines, anticipating barriers, and revising ideas and timelines. Transition team leaders can find it helpful to use the Checklist for Community Transition Steering Committees as a guide for ensuring that their work is thorough and careful (Figure A4). This guide can be particularly helpful as your team prepares to implement its plan.

SUMMARIZING THEMES

Congratulations! If you have made it this far in your work, you are well on your way to implementing a successful transition plan in your school or community. By this point you have:

- Formed a collaborative transition team and steering committee that meet regularly

- Adopted a model of transition and guiding principles for planning

- Created a Transition Practices Brainstorming Guide for ideas about transition practices that could be implemented in your school or community

- Created a Transition Timeline to use as a tool for further planning and implementation

- Tried to anticipate some of the barriers to participation by parents, teachers, and school systems

- Revised ideas and timelines to address barriers and meet challenges

Like any good plan, what you have developed as a transition plan should be treated as a work in progress even during implementation. Your regular transition team meetings are the vehicle for the implementation, evaluation, and revision of the transition plan. Once you start implementing your plan, you will hear about what works and what doesn't work, and many new ideas about ways to improve the plan and add to it will spring up. The team should use all of this information to update, revise, and improve the plan. Nothing should be set in stone! The next chapter discusses how the Transition Practices Brainstorming Guide that you created in Step 4 becomes the Transition Practices Menu that you use throughout the year as you prepare children to make the transition from preschool to kindergarten.

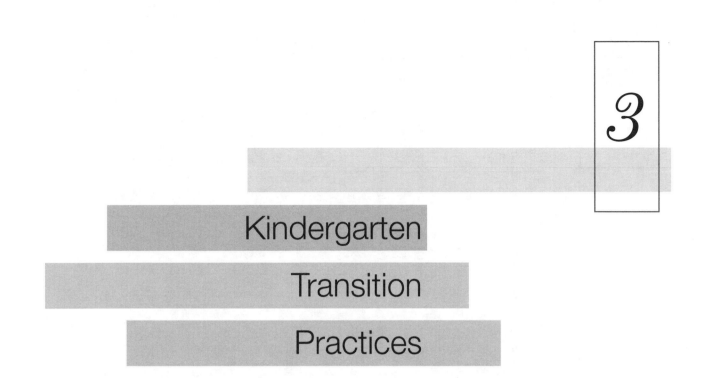

3

Kindergarten

Transition

Practices

Once the Transition Practices Brainstorming Guide is created and the Transition Timeline Worksheet has established a timeline for the transition plan, implementation can proceed. As the transition process progresses, the strategies can be fine-tuned for maximum effectiveness. Transition teams are strongly encouraged to assess the needs of both the school programs and the individual children and families in order to guide their choices in selecting transition activities. This chapter presents a detailed description of Step 8.

STEP 8   IMPLEMENT TRANSITION PRACTICES

Now that you have revised the Transition Practices Brainstorming Guide and set up a timeline, you can use them to guide your transition practices menu. Following from extensive community- and school-level transition team discussions, this menu should represent a set of transition activities that has been identified and refined, and the result is a large set of transition activities that serve as a starting point for discussions of implementation. A menu of sample transition practices is presented in this chapter in detail as a way of facilitating transition teams' discussions and generating ideas about possible transition practices (see Table 3.1). Like any good menu, this is a list of possibilities, and not all choices will appeal to everyone. We encourage transition teams to review the items, pick items that will be helpful and useful and that fit needs they have identified, and then experiment with implementing those practices.

Table 3.1. An example of a menu of transition practices

Type of connection	Menu activity	How	Who initiates	When
Family–school connections	Contact families during first few days of preschool and kindergarten	Telephone calls, visits	Teacher, principal	First week of preschool and kindergarten
	Assess family needs	Interviews	Transition coordinator	First 2 weeks of preschool and kindergarten
	Maintain periodic contact with the family	Telephone calls, notes, newsletters, home visits	Teacher, transition coordinator	Ongoing
	Connect the family to community resources	Telephone calls, notes, newsletters, home visits	Family, teacher, transition coordinator	As needed
	Encourage family participation in home learning activities	Materials and/or instructions sent home	Teacher, transition coordinator	Ongoing, particularly during summer between preschool and kindergarten
	Encourage family participation in the classroom and at school events	Telephone calls, notes, newsletters, home visits	Family, teacher, principal, transition coordinator	Ongoing, particularly at the start of the school year
	Conduct regular family meetings at school	Lunches, family nights	Teacher, principal, transition coordinator	Ongoing and at regular intervals
	Conduct family meetings about transition issues	Family nights, workshops	Transition coordinator	Preschool spring, summer, and kindergarten fall
	Coordinate sharing of information about individual children among the family, preschool teacher, and kindergarten teacher	Conferences	Transition coordinator	Preschool spring or summer
	Create newsletters and resource materials	Transition packets, tips handouts	Transition coordinator	Ongoing
	Conduct parent orientation after preschool and kindergarten start	Back-to-School nights	Principal, transition coordinator	First 2 weeks of preschool and kindergarten
Child–school connections	Establish a connection between the preschool child and kindergarten teacher	Visits to the kindergarten classroom by the child or visits by kindergarten teacher to the preschool classroom	Teachers, transition coordinator	Preschool spring
	Create a connection between the child and the kindergarten using special school functions	School fairs, assemblies, playground parties	Principals, transition coordinator	Preschool spring and summer

	Practice	Method	Personnel	Timing
	Have children practice kindergarten rituals in preschool	Practice behaviors, sing songs, read stories	Preschool teacher	Preschool spring
	Incorporate preschool activities into the kindergarten year	Read a favorite book, have similar centers	Kindergarten teacher	Kindergarten fall
	Encourage the preschool teachers to stay in contact with their former students	Letters, school visits	Teachers	Kindergarten fall
	Encourage kindergarten support staff to visit preschool children	School or home visits	School social workers, guidance counselors, transition coordinator	Preschool spring or summer
Peer connections	Establish peer connections within the preschool class	Purposeful classroom assignments	Principal, transition coordinator	Summers before preschool and kindergarten
	Establish peer connections outside of school	Play dates	Family, teachers, transition coordinator	Ongoing, particularly during the summer
	Establish connections with peers who will be in kindergarten	Activities with other preschools	Transition coordinator	Ongoing, particularly during the pre-school spring and summer
	Establish preschool peer connections with kindergarten peers	School visits, summer school	Teachers, transition coordinator	Preschool spring and summer
	Coordinate group-based peer connections	Social skills groups	Guidance counselor, transition coordinator	Kindergarten fall
Community connections	Build useful policies related to transition	Policy coordination, discussion of classroom practices	Transition coordinator administrators	Ongoing
	Foster inter-school collaboration about programs and classroom practices	Policy coordination, discussion of classroom practices	Policy makers, administrators	Ongoing
	Identify and communicate curriculum and community expectations for children	Development of goals and definition of skills	School administrators, transition coordinator	Ongoing
	Create inter-school connections about a specific child	Telephone calls, conferences	Teachers, transition coordinator	Preschool spring, summer, and kindergarten fall
	Establish policy coordination through inter-agency connections	Policy coordination, service coordination	School administrators, transition coordinator	Ongoing
	Establish child-specific coordination through inter-agency connections	Policy coordination, service coordination	School administrators, transition coordinator	Ongoing

When considering the menu presented in this chapter, it is important to note that this is an open-ended list. Teams may add their own ideas and activities to this list—we encourage you to do that. Also, it is a long list, and teams should not think that in order to have a successful transition plan they need to adopt all or even many of the items and practices listed here. This menu is presented only as another tool for transition teams working on developing plans.

Specific transition activities can be selected from the transition practices menu. This menu was developed by a collaborative transition team and has been refined and expanded over several years. It is designed to be used as an open-ended working document. Founded on the five guiding principles described in Chapter 1, this approach offers a variety of practices to promote the connections among children, families, and schools. These include family–school relationships, child–school relationships, peer relationships, and relationships between preschool and elementary schools. For families, these practices create opportunities to connect with one another and with the school. For the children, these practices foster interactions with peers who will attend their kindergarten class. Preschool children also have contact with current kindergartners who help acclimate them to the kindergarten environment. Through these contacts, children also become acquainted with their kindergarten teacher and classroom. This process of developing connections starts in preschool and is carried through to kindergarten.

School personnel may choose from the menu of activities and add their own ideas to the plan devised for a given family. The suggested activities are varied with respect to time and intensity. Some activities may affect connections on a number of levels. For example, summer playground nights for families foster family–school, child–school, and peer connections. The intensity and the number of practices implemented for each child depend on the characteristics of the child, the family, and the school. Some families require a greater level of involvement, and others need less. This approach is individually tailored for each preschool and elementary school program as well. During our implementation of this program, teachers and family workers kept track of the transition activities on the Kindergarten Transition Menu Checklist (see Chapter 4). Another way of monitoring implementation is to divide transition activities by the person responsible (e.g., teacher, principal) and to give that person a checklist that serves as a reminder of his or her commitments to the transition process. Examples of these are included in the Appendix Figures A5–A8.

In applying the various options, school personnel are encouraged to deepen connections whenever possible. If the family has the need and is receptive, a higher level of intervention is preferable and is more likely to build positive relationships between families and schools. For example, the family assessment is best accomplished through face-to-face meetings with families rather than by telephone contacts or written questionnaires. A tour of the elementary school is preferable to a note sent home to families describing the school's facilities.

Throughout this discussion, examples are given for children in preschool programs. However, the same principles are also applicable to helping children in child care make the transition. The transition coordinator or family worker is described as implementing many of the transition practices in conjunction with teachers. Again, coordination of transition activities may be done by family workers in some schools and by a counselor or teacher in others.

Table 3.1 provides a brief overview, which can be used as a tool when developing a transition plan. The complete menu can then be read for further description of the transition practices. Descriptions of each transition practice in Table 3.1 follow.

Family–School Connections

GOAL: To increase family collaboration and involvement with the school and the transition process

The relationship between the family and the child's school is invaluable in supporting positive school outcomes. Establishing this relationship at the preschool level and encouraging this relationship as the child enters school can have long-term consequences for family involvement in their child's education. Families benefit from feedback about their children and the educational services their children are receiving. Equally important is the information that schools receive from families. Both are essential components in maintaining a supportive connective loop between families and schools. This can be accomplished through interactions between an individual family with the teacher, transition coordinator, family worker, or other school personnel, or through family involvement with the school in group activities. Formal and informal meetings with teachers and the transition coordinator for mutual information sharing are avenues to promote family connections. Other avenues include meetings with other families, classroom visits, family involvement in home-based learning activities, and volunteer activities. The following are offered as suggested practices.

Contact Families During the First Few Days of Preschool and Kindergarten

The teacher or transition coordinator contacts the family for mutual information sharing. Information from the school's perspective about how the child did the first several days of school is shared. The parent is also asked how the child's and the family's initial adjustment to school has been. This can be accomplished through a telephone call or face-to-face contact.

Assess Family Needs

A transition coordinator or other program or school professional assesses the family's needs within the first 2 weeks of preschool and kindergarten and follows up as needed. The purpose of this assessment is both to make initial contact with the family and to help develop a plan of family support. This is ideally accomplished through face-to-face contact, preferably a home visit or a family school visit. Telephone contact is a less preferred option but at times may be the best alternative. This contact is coordinated with the teacher's early contact with the family and can be established during the screening process shortly before preschool or kindergarten begins. Assessments should not be duplicative but rather should help the transition coordinator establish a direct relationship with the family and determine whether concerns exist. One parent said this about the assessment:

"The prescreening thing really helped, too, because I got a chance to really sit down and talk to [the teacher] before [my son] started to let her know, you know, some things about him."

Maintain Periodic Contact with the Family

The transition coordinator maintains contact with the family during the preschool year, occasionally during the summer, and throughout the kindergarten year. Concerns are addressed as needed. For example, it might be helpful for the transition coordinator to guide families with family routines and bedtime rituals in preparation for the onset of school.

Through the transition process, each family may require a varied degree of assistance and contact. Some families may be able to negotiate the educational system quite independently. Others may have multiple needs warranting more extensive involvement. The transition coordinator helps the family to develop skills to become its own advocate. The overall goal is eventual family-initiated involvement.

At the classroom level, families' need for contact with the school may change from preschool to kindergarten. Often, however, the level of contact offered in kindergarten is significantly different from that offered in preschool. Accurately gauging how much contact a family needs or wants can be tricky:

"Last year, we had a good relationship [with the preschool teachers]. It was nice. [This year], I don't have time. I've just been busy. I just send them to school, go to work, and come home, and so I haven't been able to go over to the school like I wanted. This teacher,

this year, she don't do nothing. She has not shared views or even showed me that she interacts with the children, like you all done. I mean, she's done nothing."

Another parent acknowledges that as children mature, the intensity of contact with school can diminish. However, she would appreciate more contact than what exists:

"We don't feel like we have to talk to [the] teacher every day [because] they already grow up a lot. We still feel like it probably would be better if we can talk to the teacher every week, at least exchange a note. Twice a week [is] not like once a day."

Connect the Family to Community Resources

Families sometimes require assistance with resource needs, behavioral consultation, or other family concerns, such as dental, health, and child care. Referrals to services are provided as indicated. Facilitating contact with these services and incorporating pertinent recommendations into school programming help connect the family with the school.

Encourage Family
Participation in Home Learning Activities

The teacher and transition coordinator create learning activities for home, such as early literacy activities, sorting activities, word or letter learning games, and so forth. These activities are designed so that parents can work directly with their children. If parents are not able to visit the school, the materials can be sent home in packets for the children to work on with their families. These activities help promote family involvement and family literacy. Over the summer, specific projects might be designed for the family and child to work on together. The transition coordinator can facilitate these activities during home visits.

"[The kindergarten teachers] keep me informed about how [my daughter] does. They'll send notes home, and they sent homework for her to do that we can do together, like flash cards and word games and stuff like that. They're just real good teachers, both of them are. They let me know when they felt that she was having a problem, like keeping up with the other children and she needed to go to her speech class. [The preschool teacher] was good."

"We try to work together on stuff. Yeah, I do appreciate that. We have been very involved and connected as far as [my son] is concerned."

Encourage Family Participation
in the Classroom and at School Events

Families are encouraged to become involved in the classroom and volunteer as they are able. As the end of the school year approaches, the elementary school, kindergarten teachers, or parent–teacher organization may share information with parents about opportunities for volunteering in kindergarten.

Families' participation in schools takes many forms. Traditionally, parent involvement includes volunteering in the classroom or attending parent–teacher organization meetings. However, home activities that foster children's education, such as doing literacy activities and helping children with homework, are also within the realm of parent involvement. Parents are involved in a range of activities. They typically describe their involvement in terms of classroom visits or assistance provided on field trips:

"They've had class parties that I've been able to participate in. I haven't been able to go on any field trips. I did go on one last year. It was an all afternoon deal. I helped on that [but] I haven't really got to do a whole lot."

"I try to go to his classroom at least twice a month. [His dad] goes when he feels like it. He goes when I go but I think he also goes on a day when I don't go. He's been going on the field trips, too. They don't have as many, but he goes on them."

Conduct Regular Family Meetings at School

Regular opportunities for parents to meet with one another, have contact with the school, and discuss mutually shared concerns provide a rhythm for family connections. Parent lunches or family nights allow families to become acquainted with one another.

Organize Topic-Specific Meetings   Topics for discussion can be identified by the parents and staff. Issues such as parenting, stress management, budgeting, and children's self-esteem are possibilities. Outside speakers might address concerns, or parents might generate their own discussion. Another possibility is for parents to spend a mini-preschool day in the classroom and to role play being preschoolers.

Arrange Social Activities   Informal social activities are a means of connecting families. They might occur around a holiday (e.g., a Thanksgiving lunch for families) or a special time of year. Social activities among parents outside of school can also be fostered.

Conduct Family Meetings About Transition Issues

Meeting in the Preschool Year
Kindergarten teachers and parents of kindergartners should meet with parents of preschool children during the preschool year to share information about the kindergarten experience and to answer questions. Similarities and differences between preschool and kindergarten can be addressed. A parent–teacher organization representative could speak about how parents can be involved in this organization. This meeting can be incorporated into a regular parents' lunch or family night at the preschool. Another venue is a summer workshop for parents or an informal dinner in conjunction with schools' open houses.

Meeting Before the Onset of Kindergarten
A group meeting is held for families of preschoolers in the scheduled kindergarten classroom with the teachers to address the expectations for kindergarten and provide a tour of the elementary school. This may be incorporated into an elementary school spring orientation or school open house shortly before school starts. It may also be coordinated with the children's visit to the school.

Coordinate Sharing of Information About Individual Children Among the Family, Preschool Teacher, and Kindergarten Teacher

A particularly focused way to build connections between families and schools and establish common expectations for school is through a meeting that includes the family, the kindergarten teacher, the transition coordinator, and if applicable, the preschool teacher. In the meeting, the family and the preschool teacher share information with the kindergarten teacher about the child. The kindergarten teacher also discusses what the parent can do at home to get the child ready for school. Information discussed includes the child's interests and preferences as she or he enters kindergarten, information about the family, and any parental goals and concerns. This activity should take place in the late spring or summer and is preferably done in person rather than through written correspondence. This exchange can also be accomplished during a kindergarten screening prior to the beginning of kindergarten. Early in the kindergarten year, the family should have contact with the teacher to discuss any updated issues. This can be facilitated by the transition coordinator.

Create Newsletters and Resource Materials

Newsletters from the school program to families can provide specific information about transition-to-kindergarten issues. Important information could include springtime preparation for the transition, information on parent rights and responsibilities, and summer transition packets.

Conduct Parent Orientations after Preschool and Kindergarten Start

The school provides an orientation for parents to their child's program once school begins. This is typically accomplished through back-to-school nights but can take other formats.

"The orientation that the school gives, the spring orientation that they give when the preschools come in to visit, and then, the school orientation—the conferences are pretty late, 2 months later, but I think they're good. I think that way the teacher can tell you exactly where your child is and, you know, what they need to work on and stuff like that."

Child–School Connections

GOAL: To increase children's familiarity with the kindergarten setting

Introducing preschool children to kindergarten and kindergarten-related activities familiarizes the children with the classroom, the school environment, and their new teacher, further easing the transition process. For children who do not attend a formal preschool program, transition coordinators need to establish the types of connections listed in this section with individual or groups of families and children, usually by working through neighborhood or community services.

Establish a Connection Between the Preschool Child and Kindergarten Teacher

The preschool child gets the opportunity to interact directly with his or her anticipated kindergarten teacher through occasional visits to the kindergarten class in the spring of the preschool year. The kindergarten teacher visits the preschool classroom, or the contact can be incorporated into a kindergarten center-time or story-time activity. This is best accomplished when the class list can be established, at least on a tentative basis, for children identified for kindergarten attendance. If the teacher has been identified, this contact fosters the child's familiarity with his or her teacher. If preliminary class lists cannot be established, then the child can still benefit from visiting a kindergarten classroom.

Visits to preschool before the onset of kindergarten familiarize children with the classroom. Children who had an opportunity to participate in this activity were reported to benefit from the experience:

"She wasn't uncomfortable going. Spending the time in the classroom like they did last year, going to visit, helped a whole lot."

"I think it would be helpful to have a field trip together to see what school is like for a day."

Create a Connection Between the Child and the Kindergarten Using Special School Functions

The child visits the elementary school during a special school-wide activity. Spring fairs or special entertainment-related assemblies are possible opportunities. Spring and summer kindergarten orientation programs and a chance for children to experience their first school bus ride also help connect children to their new school. An informal summer playground time in which children can visit with their peers on the playground, have a Popsicle, and perhaps see their kindergarten teacher is an additional possibility. This is a low-key way in which children can become comfortable with school.

Have Children Practice Kindergarten Rituals in Preschool

Activities in preschool provide the child with information about kindergarten. Some of the rules and rituals of kindergarten can be practiced during the preschool day. For example, preschoolers can practice walking in a "kindergarten line," sing songs that will be sung in kindergarten, or read a special story that helps to familiarize the children with the kindergarten environment. These activities provide familiarity that can ease the transition process. In addition, once the kindergarten teacher is identified, the child can become acquainted with the teacher by reviewing the teacher's name and being shown his or her photograph. The school might develop a scrapbook of photographs from kindergarten including pictures of the teachers, the principal, the office staff, bus drivers, the classrooms, the cafeteria, the playground, and other key aspects of the school. This book can be available for children's review in the preschool class.

Incorporate Preschool Activities into the Kindergarten Year

Early in the kindergarten year, activities from preschool provide continuity for the child. These activities evoke familiar memories from preschool, which can ease the child's adjustment to the new schoolroom. For example, the child may read a favorite book from preschool or sing a special song. The kindergarten classroom may have similar centers to preschool and may offer a free-choice time for children.

Encourage Preschool Teachers to Stay in Contact with Their Former Students

The preschool teacher may visit or write letters to former students in the kindergarten classroom to ease the transition process. He or she might, for example, be an invited guest to read a story to the class or participate in a special schoolwide or classroom event early in the school year.

Encourage Kindergarten Support Staff to Visit Preschool Children

Guidance counselors, school social workers, or other kindergarten support staff visit preschoolers to learn about their particular needs. This contact establishes a connection between the child and the school before kindergarten begins. The relationship with the support staff can then be carried into the kindergarten year and provide additional support and assistance to the child and family as needs arise.

Peer Connections

GOAL: To provide children with the opportunity to engage in positive relationships with peers who can make the transition with them to kindergarten

The ability of children to get along with their peers is a major source of concern for kindergarten teachers as children begin school. As children move from preschool into kindergarten, connections between children and their peers help them feel more comfortable in their new environment and provide familiar peer experiences prior to the onset of school. These connections can be developed through links between preschool children and peers, both inside and outside the classroom; links with kindergarten peers; and links with children not enrolled in preschool who will be in their kindergarten class.

Establish Peer Connections within the Preschool Class

Assigning a child to a class with children expected to be in the same kindergarten creates opportunities for continuity of peer connections and can foster existing peer neighborhood connections as well. This connection allows the preschool child to meet and play with the same-age peers on a daily basis during the course of the school day. These interactions foster friendships that may carry into kindergarten. Children are able to practice new behaviors, and experience social problem solving and emotion regulation in a new way. If indicated, the transition coordinator can assist the teacher in the class to promote peer relationships.

Establish Peer Connections Outside of School

Peer connections outside of school are fostered with preschool friends. The transition coordinator or a teacher may help the family to arrange visits with school friends in the afternoon, during weekends, or during the summer. Summertime presents a special challenge to sustaining connections for children. Continuity of contact during the summer helps carry existing peer relationships forward into the following school year. These connections can be beneficial for families, as well as for the children.

Establish Connections with Peers Who Will Be in Kindergarten

Opportunities may be provided for the preschool child to meet and play with a child who is not in the same preschool program but who will be in the same kindergarten class. Building the natural linkages that exist for children in their neighborhood and community helps the transition process. Programs over the summer, such as prekindergarten camps, are one such opportunity. These programs offer children a chance to interact with peers who will be in their class. In addition to promoting peer connections, familiarity with the elementary school and kindergarten teachers is achieved.

Establish Preschool Peer Connections with Kindergarten Peers

A connection with current kindergarten children offers the preschool child an opportunity to learn about what to expect in kindergarten and provides a bridge for the children between the programs. The kindergarten children serve as mentors to the preschool children. This connection is accomplished in a variety of ways. The children from the two programs can interact informally or specific buddies can be identified for one-to-one interaction. Kindergartners may visit the preschool, preschoolers may visit the kindergarten, or there may be a combination of the two. This connection can be established in the spring of the preschool year.

Kindergartners Visit Preschool   Preschool children benefit from visits by kindergarten children, generally done in conjunction with a visit from the kindergarten teacher. The kindergartners can describe their experiences and answer questions from the preschool children.

Preschoolers Visit the Kindergarten Class   Interaction with elementary-age children is promoted during visits to the kindergarten classroom. During these visits, the kindergarten buddy might read a story to the preschooler, demonstrate how to play a game, show the younger child how to use the classroom computer, or interact informally on the playground. Preschool children may also eat lunch in the cafeteria with the kindergarten class. Joint field trips with the preschool and kindergarten classes provide an additional means to connect children with kindergarten peers.

Coordinate Group-Based Peer Connections

Activity-based social skills groups (generally conducted in kindergarten) can foster peer relationships. These groups are generally run with a small group of children outside the classroom.

Community Connections

GOAL: To facilitate continuity in the transition process within
       the community

In addition to family–school, child–school, and peer connections, connections at the community level between schools and other agencies serve a critical role in the transition process. These community linkages help ensure continuity for children and help provide cohesion to the services offered to children during the preschool and early elementary school years.

For example, a major discontinuity for children and families are differences in the sets of expectations between preschool and kindergarten. Kindergarten is quite different for children (e.g., more academic demands, more children, less time with teacher), and parents report that contact with the school becomes less frequent and more formalized as children go to kindergarten. These discontinuities can be smoothed out by good transition planning and communication. Transition is supported when kindergarten and preschools meet together to identify goals for children in general and when they meet to discuss individual children's needs. If the preschool program is housed in the elementary school, coordination needs to occur within the school. The challenge becomes greater when children attend a preschool or child care program independent from the elementary school or have no prekindergarten school experience. These situations require careful coordination among the programs.

Community-level coordination and communication that affect transition for children, families, and schools also are useful for promoting literacy and organizing events, such as kindergarten registration. For example, with regard to kindergarten registration, it is often the case that registration dates are announced in the local paper and about one-third to one-half of the population shows up. This in itself is a problem but also creates barriers for transition policies that try to promote contact among the child and family and the child's kindergarten teacher-to-be. Thus, community agencies and resources can band together to promote kindergarten registration instead of viewing registration as a school event. In this scenario, health care or social services agencies inform their staffs who visit families with eligible children to register them at home; television advertisements are placed announcing registration fairs; and service providers, such as pediatricians, have staff on hand to register children.

Similarly, many communities are working hard to promote literacy but often at cross purposes, thereby undermining children's capacities to acquire skills that can help them make a good transition. Schools have a set of literacy programs and expectations for children; health providers may hand out their own early literacy materials, such as "books in a bag" kits; home visitors may have yet another approach; and preschools probably do something else. It is very important that these well-intended but *different* approaches to facilitating literacy work together. Coordination and integration of these diverse efforts can only be achieved by good communication and transition planning in the community.

Effective transition experiences, therefore, are influenced not only by the relationships that teachers and other school personnel have with families but also by broader school and agency policy. Ongoing collaboration among professionals is fundamental in the development and implementation of transition practices.

Build Useful Policies Related to Transition

Community transition teams must consider the ramifications of school system policies in designing their interventions. It is equally imperative, if not more so, that schools purposefully consider the needs of the transition process in designing school policies. These policies should seek to support the key transition principles, not simply legislate particular transition programs. Furthermore, they need to capitalize on the resources already present in the system and build local support from the rest of the community. This allows the formation of the linkages described in the developmental model of transition and builds leadership and cohesion within the school community. In particular, policies should

Define and describe school readiness for children ages 2–7   Policy makers should consider what readiness means for children, families, and schools. They should outline readiness factors for children from preschool through the first grade so that transition policies address the precursors, proximal factors, and outcomes related to transition. This information should be shared with parents, teachers, and schools as part of a community awareness or public awareness initiative.

Outline state and local mandates for transition planning   Although the community transition teams specifically outline plans for their school programs, administrators should be prepared to describe the framework in which these plans will function from a policy-wide, big picture perspective. This means mandating adherence to the conceptual model, identifying key constituents who will provide support for the transition programs, naming leaders for the process, and clarifying the roles and responsibilities of the public schools.

Foster Inter-School Collaboration About Programs

Staff from the preschool and the kindergarten collaborate on placement, screening, and registration practices. For example, schools can maintain the ties between children and families by cooperating in order to ensure that children who attended preschool together can be in the same kindergarten class. Another placement consideration is arranging for a child to have the same kindergarten teacher as his or her older sibling. This can help build on existing family–school connections. Generating class lists in the spring, rather than just before the beginning of school, can lead to other practices that facilitate preschoolers' earlier connections with their kindergarten teacher.

These decisions can create challenges for school administrators in balancing the promotion of transition practices with competing demands. For example, balancing classrooms for gender, ethnicity, and achievement levels remains an important consideration in placement decisions, even in the face of the need to foster peer and family connections.

"We have this big folder if you wade through that and try to figure out some things, but it might be nice if we were just given a little background on the parents that we are asked to work with as to what their participation was. Did they participate last year? Was it a parent who didn't show for anything? A lot of times, I have to call over to [the preschool] and ask, 'What's the story?' But I don't think we should have to do that. If they want us to work with these children, I think they should give us some background."

Foster Inter-School Collaboration About Classroom Practices

The preschool teacher, kindergarten teacher, and transition coordinator meet and discuss their programs and familiarize one another about their classroom practices, traditions, and rituals. Certain activities, such as a morning meeting or a classroom management program, can be incorporated into the preschool classroom. Visits by the preschool teacher to the kindergarten and visits by kindergarten teacher to the preschool also help educators understand each other's programs. Principals, resource teachers, and counselors can participate in this process as well.

Identify and Communicate the Curriculum and Community Expectations for Children

Preschools and kindergarten programs identify and state clear expectations for children's performance and then work together to ensure that children have the opportunity to be taught the skills that meet these expectations. Defining a set or progression of skills from ages 3 to 6 and then communicating about this with the community, using language that families can understand, helps to create a skill link from preschool to kindergarten.

Create Inter-School Connections about a Specific Child

The preschool teacher, kindergarten teacher, and transition coordinator communicate about each child's needs as she or he transitions to kindergarten. Any concerns are addressed using effective strategies to manage the behavior rather than focusing on negative aspects of the child. One kindergarten teacher suggested that preschool teachers share background information about children more succinctly. The initiation of contact is viewed as the preschool's responsibility.

Establish Policy Coordination Through Inter-Agency Connections

Community agencies serving young children (e.g., child protection services, welfare programs, health programs, parenting services) coordinate services with schools to foster a smooth transition to kindergarten. The transition team or the coordinator should work with these agencies to identify their roles and tasks related to the transition plan.

Establish Child-Specific Coordination Through Inter-Agency Connections

Continuity among services is maintained through coordination with significant community agencies as the child makes the transition to school. When the transition coordinator has worked closely with a social service, health care, or mental health agency while the child has attended preschool, services are coordinated as the child enters kindergarten. The parents' consent to share information must be obtained first.

SUMMARIZING THEMES

Developing a community transition intervention entails the formation of a collaborative team with the major players in the transition process. This team needs to be established at the district and school levels. The identification of a transition coordinator, the creation of a timeline, and ongoing evaluation and revision through the implementation process are key elements of the intervention process. Developing a transition practices menu that fosters family–school, child–school, peer, and community connections offers a valuable tool for school personnel in enhancing the transition process.

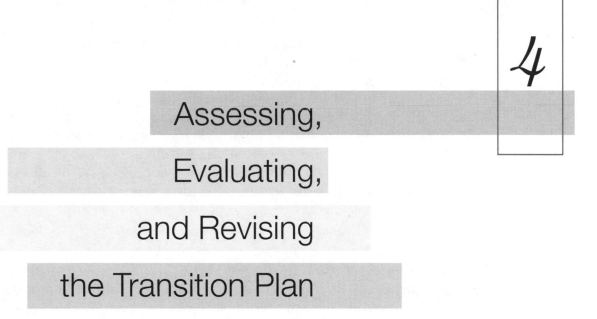

Assessing, Evaluating, and Revising the Transition Plan

4

By this point, your team has identified a team coordinator, met regularly to discuss transition issues, generated ideas for transition activities, and created a transition timeline. The team has also tried to anticipate and address any barriers, revised ideas and the timeline, and developed a menu of transition practices for the community, the schools, and individual children. So much has been accomplished, and to some, the process might seem finished; however, one crucial, continual step remains.

STEP 9   ASSESS, EVALUATE, AND REVISE

Once the transition process has been completed, transition teams need to evaluate the activities they used, identify needs that were not met, highlight the strategies that worked well, and revise future transition plans accordingly. Your collaborative team should evaluate the outcome of implementing the transition plan at the community and school levels and make necessary adjustments and changes. This is an ongoing and dynamic process. Some strategies may work well with some families but may be less effective with others. Analysis of what works and what does not can help improve the transition planning and implementation process.

Evaluation can be conducted in several ways using a variety of tools. Most important, the transition teams at the community and school levels need to solicit and be open to critical and constructive comments and input from a variety of participants in the transition process. This input can be gathered through informal conversations, focus group meetings, or more formal interviews or questionnaires. In implementing this process, we found that all of these mechanisms were helpful in providing information that was useful in further refinement and implementation of the transition plan.

The list of tools below is a sample of formal measures that can be used but are by no means essential for implementation of this approach to kindergarten transition (see Table 4.1). These evaluative tools are optional. Transition teams should choose the measures that provide the feedback most related to their specified goals and that are most informative to their decision-making process.

Kindergarten Transition Contact Log   A transition contact log can be very useful. (A sample Kindergarten Transition Contact Log is provided in Appendix Figure A9.) The team coordinator can use a contact log to track the contact maintained with school personnel. The date of contact, the person contacted, topics discussed, and the nature of the contact can be documented to get a sense of the degree to which follow-up occurred during the kindergarten year. Used in this way, a Kindergarten Transition Contact Log can help identify which children received or required the most follow-up in kindergarten and how long that level of follow-up was necessary.

The Kindergarten Transition Contact Log can also be used by team members to record their contacts with families. Information about contacts between the team member and families can be recorded, such as who was contacted, the setting, the topics discussed, and the recorder's general impression of the interaction. Used in this way, the Kindergarten Transition Contact Log can be an important tool for collecting families' specific responses to kindergarten transitions, which might not otherwise be evident or easy to elicit.

Table 4.1.   Transition evaluation instruments

Instrument	When to conduct	Who should participate
Transition Interview	Kindergarten: ongoing	Kindergarten workers, family workers
Kindergarten Transition Contact Log	Preschool: ongoing Kindergarten: ongoing	Preschool and kindergarten teachers, family workers
Kindergarten Transition Menu Checklist	Preschool: on a weekly basis Summer	Family workers
Kindergarten Transition Parent Interviews	Preschool: fall, winter, and spring Kindergarten: fall and winter	Parent/guardian
Transition Activities Questionnaires	Preschool: spring Kindergarten: fall	Preschool and kindergarten teachers, family workers, principals

Kindergarten Transition Menu Checklist The Kindergarten Transition Menu Checklist documents the use of transition practices throughout the course of preschool and the summer before kindergarten (see Figure 4.1 and Appendix Figures A10–A11). Transition participants with a role in implementation incorporate ideas from the Transition Practices Menu, along with other activities, into the transition plan for each family they follow. These professionals maintain the checklist to monitor the transition activities they coordinate. For each child, they record the week the activity occurred and whether the activity involved family–school connections, child–school connections (between the preschool child and the kindergarten), peer connections (among preschoolers or between preschoolers and kindergartners), or community connections (between schools or between the school and other agencies).

The checklists allow transition teams to monitor both the frequency and intensity of transition connections for each child, and to do so over time. Data can also be compiled according to the transition coordinator to monitor differences between programs or schools.

Kindergarten Transition Parent Interviews Kindergarten Transition Parent Interviews serve the dual purpose of engaging families in relationships with schools and gathering information about family experiences in schools and at home. (Samples are provided in Appendix Figures A12–A13.) Transition coordinators can conduct the interviews with parents or guardians, generally in families' homes. The interviews are typically completed in September, February, and May during the preschool year and in September and February during the kindergarten year. The interviews focus on parents' descriptions of their child's school experiences, child behavior, routines in preparing for school, family relationships with schools, and peer contact outside of school.

In addition to these general themes, each interview should be tailored to seasonal issues. For example, the preschool fall interview can include questions about activities that parents did with their children to prepare for preschool. This interview also serves as the assessment tool for identifying a family's strengths and needs. The spring preschool interview includes questions about parents' satisfaction with the preschool program, parent involvement with the preschool, and family activities in preparation for kindergarten. The fall kindergarten interview addresses families' summer preparations for school asking parents to reflect on their families' experiences with the transition process.

These interviews provide a window into parents' perceptions about their role in supporting transition and other school activities. The interviews generate detailed information about the child's life outside of school, including specific home activities, household stressors, and peer relationships. In several

Kindergarten Transition Menu Checklist

Directions: Check as many boxes as apply.   Week of ___August 10___

Student	Family–school activities	Child–school contact	Preschool peer contact	Kindergarten peer contact	Community contact	Description of activity
LeRoy Johnson		✓		✓		Visit to elementary school
Rob Wilkes	✓				✓	Met with parent coordinator to talk about transition
Natalie Vales			✓		✓	African American Heritage Festival field trip
Shaniqua Taylor			✓	✓	✓	Field day with kindergarteners
Abby Friedel	✓				✓	Meeting with elementary school principal to plan activities

Figure 4.1. A completed example of a Transition Practices Menu Checklist.

experiences with using these interviews, school staff found it helpful to gather the information and then talk to the parent about his or her responses. The interviewer discussed with the parents any areas of concerns noted in their responses and made referrals when appropriate. Interviewers using these materials must be experienced in talking to families and must be very respectful of families' privacy.

Transition Activities Questionnaires   The Transition Activities Questionnaires identify team members' experiences with various transition activities. (Sample questionnaires can be found in Appendix Figures A12–A13.) Preschool and kindergarten teachers, principals, transition coordinators, and parents respond to questions concerning specific transition activities, the usefulness of the activities, and barriers to transition practices. School personnel complete these questionnaires in the spring of preschool, and kindergarten teachers complete them in the fall to ascertain any additional activities they engaged in during the summer or the beginning of kindergarten. These questionnaires provide considerable information about how often practices were used, the helpfulness of those practices, and the factors that limit or inhibit school personnel and parents from participating in transition activities. Transition teams are encouraged to create their own questionnaires to reflect the transition activities they have chosen to do but are welcome to use the samples if they are relevant. There are several versions of this questionnaire to accommodate the different roles served by members of the transition team:

• The Transition Activities Questionnaires for Preschool Teachers, Kindergarten Teachers, Transition Coordinators, Principals, and Parents are completed in the spring of the preschool year in order to understand activities that occurred during the preschool year.

• An additional Transition Activities Questionnaire for Kindergarten Teachers is completed in the fall of kindergarten in order to capture any activities that occurred over the summer and during the beginning of kindergarten.

Transition Interview   A Transition Interview has been designed to elicit team members' impressions of the transition process and their reflections on elements that may have helped or hindered the process (see Appendix Figure A1). In addition to using this interview during the needs assessment process, it can be administered in the spring of the kindergarten year. This interview provides information about the experiences of parents and school personnel after the transition process has been completed.

SUMMARIZING THEMES

By now, you are fairly familiar with the basic theory supporting effective transitions and the nine steps that move theory into actions linking families, children, and schools. When implemented, these nine steps can be effective for creating supportive transitions for children. In the next chapter, we describe how these steps were implemented with more than 100 children and families. These lessons from the field help round out the discussion and provide key examples as you design and implement this approach in your school and community.

5

Lessons

from the Field

Since 1998, our approach to transition planning has been field tested, evaluated, and refined in a number of community-, school-, and even state-level efforts to enhance transition outcomes for children, families, and schools. Our experiences and the experiences of diverse teams are described in this chapter to give you a sense of how this approach has evolved and the potential effect of this method of transition planning on communities, schools, teachers, families, and children. This developmental approach to transition can be applied to a range of community needs and can be readily tailored to specific schools and families.

The settings in which this approach has been field-tested include

1. Two very differently organized programs for preschoolers at high risk and the two school systems served by these programs. One program was an in-school prekindergarten program and the other was a centralized system-wide prekindergarten that served all of the elementary school catchment areas in the district.

2. Three states that are moving strategically and purposefully to address readiness and transition issues at the state level. In each case, the developmental approach to transition was introduced to key providers and constituents (e.g., state Department of Education personnel, Head Start personnel, principals and superintendents, Title I directors) at a state-level meeting. These personnel followed up with individual communities to begin the process of transition planning at the local level.

3. Two large, urban communities with very high rates of child poverty and non–English-speaking families. In both of these communities, a commitment to providing early childhood services was in place, and leadership was behind early childhood services in the schools and in the community. There was a noticeable degree of fragmentation and need for coordination and integration of services across preschool providers and between preschool providers and the school system. In these communities, this approach was implemented through district- and community-wide meetings of key constituencies.

CHILD CHARACTERISTICS

In most cases in which this approach has been implemented, the efforts have focused on helping children from economically or socially disadvantaged circumstances who were very likely to show high rates of failure in the early years of school. Implementation of the developmental approach to transition was viewed as an integral component of a comprehensive early intervention/ prevention initiative aimed at improving children's chances of succeeding in kindergarten. However, communities and state-wide applications have found that this approach to transition planning and implementation is effective for *all* children and families they serve. Many school districts find it best to apply this approach district-wide.

THE COLLABORATIVE TEAMS

In all cases, we developed a strategic partnership with local schools. A collaborative team—composed of family workers, preschool teachers, kindergarten teachers, principals, parents, and facilitators (either our own staff or a local leader)—was established nearly a year before intervention with families and schools took place. Members of this team met regularly to identify community needs related to the transition to kindergarten, develop the menu-based approach for their needs, and oversee the implementation process. Discussions focused on existing transition practices, ideal practices, and barriers to these practices. Through this collaboration, the team formulated programmatic changes to apply within their own programs or schools or school districts. Each program or school then implemented various transition practices geared to the specific needs of the families and schools. In addition to families, teachers, and principals, several other people played key roles in the transition process. (The following sections describe implementation on the school level, so each role is described in that context.)

Transition Coordinators

As noted in Step 2, every transition team needs to identify a coordinator or facilitator. As the school-level teams met, they needed to identify a transition coordinator for each school who would be responsible for ensuring the implementation of the transition plan in that school catchment areas.

In one area, the family workers employed at the preschool programs coordinated the transition plan from preschool through the kindergarten year for each family and school they served. The family workers' role was twofold. As preschool staff charged with providing services to families, they often tried to engage families in positive relationships with school, conduct regular home visits, connect families to community resources, and provide opportunities for involvement in parent groups in preschool. Their familiarity with the programs and families created a greater level of sensitivity and relevance in the development and implementation of transition practices. As transition coordinators for the schools they served, they also worked with kindergarten staff and preschool staff to facilitate joint meetings about curricula (or individual children), coordinated the kindergarten registration process, facilitated the assignment of children to classrooms, and provided information about issues of mutual interest across preschool and kindergarten.

For the preschool programs housed within the elementary schools, the family workers continued to follow the same families through elementary school. Continuity was quite easy to maintain in these schools. At the centralized preschool program, a teacher at one of the participating elementary schools served as the transition coordinator for that school and became involved with the children at the preschool whom she anticipated would attend the elementary school where she taught. Her links to that school enabled her to make the connections between families and the school more easily. For other children in the centralized program, the preschool family workers served this function. Thus, the coordination role was implemented in a variety of ways in different contexts due to local constraints, yet in each case, the five guiding principles were used to inform decisions and practices.

THE IMPLEMENTATION PROCESS

This approach has been field-tested in a variety of settings at different levels, although this chapter focuses on implementation at the local school level. What follows is a presentation of numerous examples, with descriptions of the actual experiences of the people involved and the implementation process. The presentation is organized into sections on the collaborative process and then specific descriptions of activities and experiences that occurred as the

Transition Timeline was implemented during the year, starting with the fall of the preschool year, one year before the children were to enter kindergarten.

Ongoing Collaboration

Throughout the implementation process, ongoing collaborative team meetings were held to discuss the transition process as it unfolded. Transition coordinators met regularly to share ideas about transition practices in their individual programs. They also met with preschool teachers, kindergarten teachers, and principals to coordinate transition activities tailored to the children's and schools' needs. Parents collaborated with transition coordinators and teachers about the transition activities in which they participated.

Comments from participants in this process reveal the importance of communication, sharing information, finding common ways to look at transition, and the value of collaboration for the building of an effective, cohesive transition plan.

One family worker stated, "Information about curriculum, children, and kindergarten placement is discussed among preschool and kindergarten staff. Teachers are very supportive of this process and have developed good relationships."

One principal reported, "Participation in the transition project enabled me to enter a dialogue with other practitioners on an important topic that is often ignored. We have known for some time we needed to deal with transition but we didn't know what to do. Having a common frame of reference was essential."

One family worker said, "The partnership with other teachers and staff provided professional stimulation and a sense of direction in my work."

In addition to ongoing collaboration, particular activities that fostered the transition process occurred during the course of the preschool and kindergarten year. These are described in the following sections.

Fall Preschool Year   In fall of the preschool year, as the participating child entered preschool, the family worker visited with the family and focused on building a relationship with them, providing support, and creating a link with the child's preschool teacher. An assessment of the child's and family's needs was done by the family worker early in the preschool year. This assessment was generally conducted through a home visit. However, if this was not possible, assessments at school or at the parent's workplace were options. During an extended interview with each parent on her caseload, the family worker assessed a family's concerns, strengths, stressors, and perceptions about school through specifically focusing on the needs of the preschool child. One family worker reported that the home visits "opened the doors for communication since the focus was on the children and not adult failures."

The family worker referred the family to appropriate community agencies, as indicated. The child's preschool teacher also contacted the parents within the first week of school to find out about how the family felt the child's initial adjustment had been. Ongoing parent involvement was encouraged through regular parent meetings coordinated by the family worker. Preschool programs also offered opportunities for parents to become involved in learning activities at home. In addition to family involvement, the teacher, through the normal course of the preschool day, fostered peer interaction in the classroom among children who were expected to attend the same kindergarten. The overall goal of all these actions was to build a strength-based relationship between the school and family in which the child and his or her parents felt valued and supported and the teacher had an effective communication link with the parents.

In terms of communication between schools and families, most school personnel indicate that developing relationships with parents is critical in children's school success. Teachers and administrators generally value their communication with parents. Preschool teachers' relationships with children and their families are viewed as central to children's school adjustment:

"The school–home connections and parents feeling that you're really, really interested in the well-being of their child are going to be the things that help children be most successful."

Two kindergarten teachers reported that these relationships should be promoted with personal connections and a welcoming attitude:

"The parent interviews we do that first week are really key, because it's a time when we have a positive interaction with the parent here at school and that can set the stage for positive interaction during the year."

"You can let parents know that they are not really guests when they come here, that they are really part of the community and they can come in and see what their child is doing and do it alongside them, if they feel like it."

Elementary school principals indicated that schools have a responsibility to motivate parents to be actively involved. These relationships should be established in preschool and maintained as children enter kindergarten:

"If we can get the parents interested and involved early, they're not intimidated by school. Once they enter the public kindergarten system, all of a sudden, I think parents have somewhat of a pull-back. I'm not as overly concerned about the children as I am about the parents."

Providing opportunities for family involvement early in the school year and early in a child's school career may foster more positive perceptions by families and school personnel and may lay the groundwork for ongoing collaboration throughout the transition process.

Spring Preschool Year   In the spring, the family worker continued to facilitate regular family contact with the preschool, and efforts shifted to more formal transition activities and practices. The family worker began to establish the linkages with the anticipated kindergarten classroom. When possible, the child's kindergarten teacher was chosen. For some children, this decision could not be made until late summer. Children who were not yet assigned a kindergarten teacher had general exposure to kindergarten until the actual kindergarten teacher was determined. Once the kindergarten teacher was identified, relationships with this teacher were promoted.

Connections were expanded on a number of levels. Connections for the child with preschool peers were supplemented by connections with kindergarten peers. Each preschool child was also connected with his or her anticipated kindergarten teacher and school. Preschool and kindergarten staff met, and the family developed connections with the kindergarten teacher.

In terms of child linkages, the preschoolers gained familiarity with kindergarten through opportunities to interact with current kindergartners and with their anticipated kindergarten teacher. These connections occurred in the preschool classroom, as well as through experiences in the kindergarten classroom. Kindergarten children shared their experiences with the preschool children and were paired with preschoolers during classroom visits to read a story, play a game, or demonstrate the use of the class computer.

During the spring, it was easy to see the enthusiasm and anxiety about entering kindergarten start to build among everyone: children, parents, and teachers.

One child said, "I get to go visit my new big school today!"

One mother stated, "It really helped to see the school and kindergarten classroom so that I know what to expect. My son loved visiting the playground."

One preschool teacher remarked, "It's been great having the children spend time in the kindergarten classroom. Preschool children talk about what the kids say a lot."

One kindergarten teacher said, "Visiting the kindergarten class helps the preschoolers become more comfortable with a new class and teacher."

One principal said, "Spending time in kindergarten minimizes anxiety for preschool children."

In early spring, the family worker and preschool teacher met with the kindergarten teacher to talk about their programs and to familiarize each other with their classroom practices. Specific kindergarten activities or rituals, such as walking in a kindergarten line, reading a special story, or singing a particular song, were identified. These activities were practiced in preschool. Also, the preschool program shared activities from their program with the kindergarten teacher that could serve as a bridge of familiarity for each child when he or she entered kindergarten. Singing a familiar song or reading a favorite story from preschool helped ease the transition. As summer approached, some preschool staff discussed skill-based literacy materials with the kindergarten teacher that families could use at home during the summer.

The family worker collaborated with the family about the transition process. The family members were approached as partners in the process, experts in their own right on their child's abilities and needs. The discussion focused on expectations for kindergarten and the family's goals and concerns about their child. This meeting laid the groundwork for a conference later in the spring with the parent, kindergarten teacher, preschool teacher, and family worker.

The family had opportunities to meet as a group and individually with the anticipated kindergarten teacher in late spring. A group meeting with the kindergarten teacher during a spring orientation helped familiarize families with the expectations for kindergarten. If the teacher had not yet been identified, then a meeting with a kindergarten teacher in the spring was followed by a meeting with the actual teacher at the school's open house shortly prior to the beginning of school. When possible, the family had an opportunity to meet with the kindergarten teacher, the preschool teacher and the family worker specifically about their child.

At this meeting, the family shared information with the kindergarten teacher about their child's interests and preferences, as well as any concerns. The preschool teacher shared information about his or her experiences with the child. The kindergarten teacher in conjunction with the other participants discussed how these issues might be addressed in the kindergarten year.

Summer Before Kindergarten   In the summer before kindergarten, the family worker checked in with the child and family and addressed transition issues. If indicated, the family worker facilitated social opportunities with peers or encouraged visits to the school playground to increase familiarity with the new setting. For example, one program offered a playground "Popsicle Night" for the rising kindergartners and their families. This low-key activity enabled the families to experience school in an enjoyable and relaxed manner. In addition, the family worker provided home visits to support school adjustment through literacy activities and help with establishing family routines, such as bedtime and awakening rituals. If the elementary school had an orientation during the summer, the family worker facilitated family participation. Families were encouraged to continue working with their children around transition issues. In the fall of the kindergarten year, they were asked to describe the transition-related activities in which they participated with their child over the summer. These results are presented in Table 5.1.

Fall Kindergarten Year   In the fall of the kindergarten year, as the child began kindergarten, the family worker served as a bridge for the family into school and as a resource to the kindergarten teacher. The worker continued to encourage family involvement and monitor family adjustment. In the first 2 weeks of kindergarten, the family worker followed up to see how the child and family adjusted to kindergarten. This contact was either in person or by telephone. The family worker also checked in with the kindergarten teacher early in the school year to determine whether there were concerns warranting her attention. If a meeting had not yet occurred between the family and kindergarten teacher, this connection was established. At this time, the family shared information about their child, which helped establish a positive tone in the relationship. As in preschool, the family worker was available to address family concerns and act as a liaison between the parent and teacher. The family worker worked closely with the

Table 5.1.   Transition activities that families did with their children during the summer between preschool and kindergarten

Category	Activity	Percentage of parents and families participating
Preparing the child for kindergarten by teaching school-related skills	Practiced daily routines of getting ready for school	86
	Taught the child how to tie his or her shoe	81
	Taught the child his or her address	69
	Taught the child his or her telephone number (if applicable)	67
Preparing for kindergarten as parents and families	Talked with family members or friends who have school-age children	90
	Talked with other parents of children from the child's new school	85
Orienting the child to school	Discussed behavior expectations with the child	95
	Discussed meeting new classmates with the child	92
	Discussed with the child what will happen on the first day of school	88
	Discussed the nature of school work with the child	86
	Discussed with the child meeting the new teacher	84
	Attended the school's open house	58
	Took the child to play on the playground	56
	Read stories to the child about starting kindergarten	41

teacher, school guidance counselor, and other staff to coordinate their individual roles.

As the kindergarten year progressed, the family worker maintained regular contact with the family and teacher and fostered the connections for the child as needed. Many families were quite independent and self-sufficient in their relationships with the schools. These families required minimal intervention. Others required some assistance in negotiating the education system. Because families had opportunities for ongoing involvement with the school—starting in preschool and continuing into kindergarten—they became increasingly comfortable with the school. This led to a reduced need for family worker involvement. Families were encouraged to take more responsibility for negotiating their relationships with their child's school, thereby allowing the family worker to gradually taper her involvement.

There was variability in the experiences of teachers when the preschool program was housed in the elementary school, as opposed to in its own building. Teachers in both settings viewed the preschoolers' visits to the kindergarten classroom in the spring as beneficial:

"They know where to go that first day, they know who their teacher is, where their things are, where they are sitting. It's not such a shock."

However, teachers in elementary schools in which the preschool programs were also housed noted the added value of this characteristic in promoting children's familiarity with school:

"I think the children are a lot more comfortable. You don't have that transition month to go through at the beginning of the school year because you've met the children, they've been in our classrooms, they've been through rules and regulations of the school, and they've already met half of the children that they'll be with the next year [because we have a K–1 combination], so they build the relationships early."

This focus on how good transition practices save time in getting to know the children and families is a key element of effective practices. These practices allow information to be exchanged between home and kindergarten and between kindergarten and preschool in such a way that parents do not have to wait until the November conference for information about their child. More important, if a child is having a difficulty, the parent and teacher have an effective way of problem solving.

An elementary school principal described the benefits of having the preschool in the elementary school as a means of providing continuity and familiarity for children:

"The [preschool] children are treated just like our kindergarten classes. They move around the building, the expectations are clear, the [preschool] teacher knows what the curriculum is for the kindergarten so they can kind of feed into that and match up with that. I think it is just a continuation. Once they enter this building, it takes the child where they are and takes them as far as they can get by the time they leave. It's just help-ful to have it in the school."

For preschool programs housed in elementary schools, family workers note the benefits of continuity between programs. These family workers view this feature as a central ingredient to successful transition:

"Just having the preschool program here is probably 98% of why they made a good transition. They're going through the halls, learning hall behavior, since basic behaviors are a big part of doing okay in kindergarten."

"Having the preschool program in the school was the number one factor. Having that, they started the process immediately from day one, and just having the connection with the kindergarten teacher, whether it was the preschool teacher and the kindergarten teacher or the children and the kindergarten teacher."

OVERALL EXPERIENCES

Nearly all participants who have field-tested this approach, regardless of their professional role, acknowledge a shift in approaches and expectations as a consequence of the collaborative process the approach requires. As a consequence, relationships among kindergarten teachers, family workers, and principals tend to be more positive and supportive, and programming is more cohesive and integrated across preschool and school.

One major hurdle to overcome in good transition planning is the fact that kindergarten and preschool teachers relate to one another in different ways. Preschool teachers are often expected to accommodate the needs of kindergarten. Kindergarten teachers believe that this promotes continuity between the programs. Some kindergarten teachers suggest that preschool programs should focus more on academic skills. But preschool teachers often feel frustrated; they sense that someone is telling them what to do and that these suggestions violate their values about what kind of support young children need in the classroom. These two conflicting perspectives can be a stumbling block to building an integrated curriculum and effective communication across preschool and kindergarten; it is essential that these differences be reconciled so that effective transition planning can occur. General attitudes about families vary among school personnel, depending on the nature of their relationships with them. Although both preschool and kindergarten personnel may become frustrated with parents' limitations, when schools have more ongoing informal relationships with families, they are able to be more empathetic toward them. Because the academic demands and formal expectations of parents are generally less in preschool than in kindergarten, preschool teachers and family workers may have greater opportunities for understanding family issues. Often, appreciation of families' stresses and constraints can promote a more sensitive attitude toward them. In addition, families become more involved with the school as their children make the transition to kindergarten.

The dramatic differences in philosophical approaches from preschool into kindergarten clearly affects the communication process and relationships among preschools, kindergartens, and families. When the connections among them are fortified, the transition process is eased. Collaboration among teachers, principals, and family workers, in which these differences are openly discussed, can help families connect with schools in positive ways.

Family Experiences

The parents who participated in this approach indicated clearly that they valued assistance during the transition process because they recognized it as a potentially difficult time in the school experience, both for them and for their child. Parents generally found that participating in transition activities was helpful. As can be seen in Table 5.2, when families used the opportunities offered by the school, they overwhelmingly found them to be useful.

Parents value not only their children being familiar with the expectations for kindergarten but also knowing the expectations themselves. In addition, they like to become acquainted with the teacher and the school prior to their

Table 5.2. Transition activities that families participated in and found useful

Transition activity	Percentage of families participating	Percentage of families who used the activity and found it helpful
Having the child visit a kindergarten classroom	96	99
Meeting with a kindergarten teacher who is going to be the child's teacher	80	89
Meeting with the elementary school principal	79	95
Taking a tour of the school	78	100
Talking with preschool staff about kindergarten	76	99
Visiting the kindergarten classroom	68	97
Talking with other parents of the child's classmates	68	97
Participating in elementary schoolwide activities	58	100
Attending a workshop for parents	45	98
Meeting with the child's anticipated kindergarten teacher	38	92
Attending an orientation to kindergarten	31	96

child's school entry. Knowing, for example, specific academic expectations in kindergarten and registration requirements is considered useful. Previous experience with the school through one's own experiences or having another child attending the school also helps.

"I think he felt comfortable. I would have liked to have known what was required of him before he went to kindergarten. Then, there were some things that I could have worked on with him. When they did the screening, I found out he didn't know a lot of stuff that he should have known before going into kindergarten. If I had known that, then I could have worked with him with him beforehand."

"I already know what to expect with [her sister]. I guess once you have one child in school, you become very familiar with what you have to do to get other children in school."

One interesting insight was that the parents interviewed addressed not only transition activities offered by schools but also parents' role in the transition process. Many parents see the transition process as a two-way street. Although schools should provide opportunities for transition activities, parents have a responsibility as well. Not only do school personnel express this sentiment on occasion, but parents also acknowledge this. Parents' attitude about school, regardless of their own childhood experiences of school, is an important aspect of the transition process:

"I never liked school. I don't have good memories of school. But I push that school is important for them. My motivation is that my kids need their education and its my job to make sure that they get it, school doesn't really make a difference."

The vast majority of parents experience positive relationships with both their kindergarten and preschool teachers. Parents experience these relationships as satisfying for a number of reasons, including the teacher's availability for ongoing contact, a demonstration of genuine concern for the children, teacher sensitivity to family concerns, prior familiarity with the teacher, and effective use of notes and other modes of contact. Many parents value ongoing communication with teachers. They like to hear both positive feedback and concerns so that they know about their child's progress. Parents appreciate the ability to readily talk with their children's teachers:

"Keeping me informed of how [my child is] doing. I talk to [the teacher] all the time. She always has an answer. His preschool teacher kept in contact with me, too."

"If there is ever a problem with something that got missing from his book bag, she'll call me at home or I'll contact her—so the relationship is wonderful. I have no problems with her. I think she's a wonderful teacher. [My child] loves her."

"Oh, we get along great. She [the teacher] tells me what's going on with him and keeps me informed of every little thing that he does. She keeps a list of everything that he does and writes in a little booklet that he has there. At conference time, she showed me his progress and the stuff that he's been doing, and so I think she's wonderful."

Parents reported that their children generally have both positive academic and social adjustment to school. Ninety percent of parents reported that their children's experience in kindergarten has been good, and only 3% reported that they have concerns. Seven percent reported that their children's social adjustment has been mostly successful in kindergarten; overall, 96% report that their child's social adjustment has gone well.

When asked to elaborate on their responses, parents focused on their children's academic and social adjustment. Some parents are impressed with their children's new academic skills:

"She gets more into learning, the activity that you do. Back then [in preschool] she was drawing letters and shapes, now she's getting more things to do, more to learn, than she got in preschool. She likes to be busy, so there's more things to keep her busy. Instead of just playing all the time. Yeah, the busier she keeps, she loves to learn. It made it easy for me."

"I see him just being able to count more. Just little odds and ends. He's writing his name better."

The learning process also extends to social learning. The development of skills at school affects children's skills at home. One parent describes how she values her daughter's progress in this area.

"I'm just happy to see her progress. I think she is developing into an individual. And it's good for her. And she's getting concepts of right and wrong. Concepts of time. And she understands right and wrong behavior. So it's more easy to handle her."

Peer adjustment is also viewed as an important aspect of the transition into school for parents. Positive peer relationships can foster children's school adjustment.

"She's made good friends again and she likes school itself—so that's gone well. And she still likes everybody. You really have to do something for her to not like you, for she still likes everybody."

Other parents appreciate their child's new level of maturity, self-sufficiency, and independence. Increased maturity and encouragement by families and schools foster children's transition. This promotes children's confidence and has secondary benefits for parents because their children depend less on their parents to meet their needs.

"It's kind of maturing her a little bit. She's coming out of that baby stage and into a child stage. She doesn't depend on us as much now. And even with tying her shoes, she can do it herself. In a way, it's a relief for me, and in another way it's, oh, she's my baby. So, it's good, it's been good for me, and it's been good for her. Kind of gives me a little more time, too, because I don't have to spend so much time doing those little toddler things, trying to get through that and the other two kids, too."

School Perspectives

In general, the kindergarten teachers viewed children's adjustment at the time they enter kindergarten as a key factor in the transition from preschool. The kindergarten environment is the central context (environmental input model). Teachers vary in their recognition of preschool experiences and family influences on children's transition into kindergarten and overall adjustment to school. For some, these experiences directly connect to the transition process (developmental model). For others, adjustment relates to the quality of the kindergarten classroom instead of prior home and preschool experiences.

Preschool teachers who were interviewed overwhelmingly view school transition to be a concern for children *prior* to their entering kindergarten. Perhaps because preschool teachers have an existing relationship with their students, they are more invested in children's transition into school. Kindergarten teachers have not yet established relationships with the children and are understandably focused on their current kindergarten students. This may, in part, account for their different perspectives. For preschool teachers, transition is considered to be an important developmental, relationship-based process. One of the primary indications that children have had a successful transition into school is the development of self-confidence, self-reliance, and problem-solving skills.

Principals note the value of children developing a relationship with kindergarten teachers and becoming familiar with the school. This perspective of relationships developing over time fits the developmental approach to transition. One preschool principal stated,

"Visiting a couple times into the classroom, hopefully the classroom they would be in the next year, so the child and the family get familiar with that teacher a little earlier [helps children make the transition]."

Despite this variability in perspectives, most preschool and kindergarten teachers agree that when they participate in transition activities, these activities are useful (see Table 5.3).

RELATIONSHIPS AMONG SYSTEMS

Over the course of the intervention period, we detected a number of themes and common experiences that can be instructive in planning other transition programs. Perspectives on the relationships among systems depend on how the participants view the interactions in the transition process—the family, the preschool program, the elementary school, and the community. What are the properties of these relationships, and how do they connect with one another?

Table 5.3. Transition activities that preschool and kindergarten teachers participated in and found helpful

Kind of transition activity	Transition activity	Percentage of preschool teachers participating	Percentage of preschool teachers who found the activity useful	Percentage of kindergarten teachers participating	Percentage of kindergarten teachers who found the activity helpful
P to K	Preschool children visiting a nonspecific kindergarten classroom	100	100	74	99
	Preschool children visiting their specific kindergarten classroom	50	100	77	96
	Preschool teachers visiting a kindergarten classroom	90	100	52	100
	Holding a spring orientation about kindergarten for preschool children	60	100	41	91
K to P	Kindergarten teachers visiting a preschool classroom	20	100	19	100
	Elementary school children visiting a preschool classroom	40	100	3	50
	Holding an elementary school-wide activity with preschool children	60	83	65	100
Parent–school	Having a spring orientation about kindergarten for parents of preschool children	50	100	58	100
	Having an individual meeting between a teacher and a parent of the preschool child	50	100	23	100
School–school	Sharing written records	60	100	26	100
	Preschool and kindergarten teachers meeting about specific children	40	100	55	100
	Preschool teachers meeting with kindergarten teachers about curricula	20	100	35	100

Are there common goals among the systems? What is the nature of the dynamics and feedback loops? Does a hierarchy exist, and if so, how is this manifested? What is the participants' sense of who adapts to whom in their working relationships? What are the participants' overall attitudes and judgments about their relationships with others involved in the transition process? School personnel perspectives about these relationships can be understood in terms of two overriding themes. First, there is a shift in the expectations for children and families from preschool to elementary school. Second, the nature of the communication process among preschools, kindergartens, and families is seen by many as problematic, particularly when there is a weak link between the preschool and kindergarten programs. The interaction among teachers, principals, families, and family workers over time gives rise to their expectations and communication processes.

Shift in Expectations

Kindergarten teachers, preschool teachers, principals, and family workers reported a substantial difference in the cultures and expectations between preschool and kindergarten. Kindergarten has a greater academic focus and a more structured atmosphere, whereas preschool focuses more on development. Class sizes are generally larger in kindergarten, and there are more transitions throughout the school day. This shift creates a challenge in relationships between preschool and elementary schools, as well as between schools and families. One kindergarten teacher described this change for children:

"In kindergarten, expectations are much greater because there's a lot more of the academics, whereas in preschool, there's a lot more play opportunities and more social issues. As much as we try to hold on to that, the pressure gets to be greater when [the children] come here. The rules begin to get a little stricter and tighter."

One preschool teacher describes the multiple transitions that children face during the school day as they enter kindergarten:

"A primary barrier or difficulty is the additional class transitions that each child must get accustomed to, like music, art, library, gym, and computer lab. The often larger group size and school size is also a big change."

This principal also points to the dramatic change for children as they enter kindergarten:

"Our students have to hit the ground running because the expectations are much harder—academics—and really we need to be pushing more and we're pushing it down into [preschool]. They're doing more with letter and sound recognition, counting the numbers and matching up."

The expectations for families' relationships with schools also shift with the transition from preschool to kindergarten. Ongoing relationships with families are an integral part of children's preschool education. Although kindergarten teachers also value their relationships with families, the nature of these relationships changes. Family workers, as parent advocates and as the link between the preschool and kindergarten, echoed these parent concerns and offered a unique perspective on these relationships:

"[The parents] receive a general information sheet about what's going on [in kindergarten]. But they never hear specifically how their child is doing. Unless there's a problem, they don't get personal notes. [The kindergarten teachers] don't have the time to do personal journals every day. They just don't feel as open and the parents have stated that in [preschool] anytime they wanted to come into the classroom, whether it was just a pop-in visit or to read a story, or to come to a play, it was very open and very welcomed. Yet, they don't feel like they can just pop into kindergarten. They feel that the day is much more structured with academics and so a pop-in just doesn't fit. That's their mode of operation."

Kindergarten teachers attribute the shift in their expectations about parent relationships in kindergarten to a number of constraints. Because of larger class sizes, a greater academic focus, and more school transitions during the school day, kindergarten teachers are less able to intensively reach out to parents. This requires parents to take greater initiative in contacting the school. This can be challenging for some parents who feel intimidated by calling the school. Another issue for some parents is making the separation from their children in accordance with the rules and expectations of the school. Although this issue is not raised by preschool teachers, several kindergarten teachers mention separation difficulties. These are generally viewed as more of a concern for the parents than for the children:

"It's not usually the kids, it's usually the other way around, and sometimes with the kids when the parents expect them to have separation anxiety, then the kid kind of adopts it. So for the first week or so, they can come in and drop them off, but I try to encourage the parents to kind of cut the ties fairly soon."

"A lot of times, we tell the parents to put them on the bus from the start; of course, a lot of parents want to bring them to the door. Parents have a hard time. Some of them, they

crack the door. I've had to call up parents and say, 'Your child is fine.' But as a parent, I would probably want to take my kid, too. Then, you have parents [who] have been at the door crying."

"We're less interested in letting parents know about things, we're less caring about their individual child because—and I don't think that's true at all, but I think that may be the flavor they get because there is more of a separation [than there was in preschool]."

"It's not so bad walking them to the room, but it's once they get there, they need to say their goodbyes at the door and be ready to go. It's not that we don't want the parents in, but the child needs to know that this is school time and Mommy is going."

"I think parent interaction can be a big barrier, because if you don't get the kind of support you're looking for in that, if they continue to baby the child at home, or they continue to call, or they continue to do things like that even after you talk to them about it and said, 'It would be better if you drop them off at the office instead of bring them down to the room.' Then, they have this big separation scene or if you've asked them to make sure they do their homework independently at home, and they still do the homework for the child. It makes it hard because then they come to school and we expect them to do those things and they can't because they are not used to it."

Relationships between preschool and kindergarten teachers are also affected by the cultural change from preschool and kindergarten. Some preschool teachers view their relationship with kindergarten teachers as strained due to a difference in expectations. This preschool teacher expressed frustration with the differences in approaches between the programs:

"I'm really well aware of what kindergarten expectations are. I don't think a lot of those expectations are developmentally appropriate. When we have children coming into a classroom who have no speech, don't know how to flush, don't know how to wipe, don't know how to wash their hands, cannot function in a routine, the last thing in the world I'm going to do is start on phonemic awareness. They may or may not get that for the entire year if it takes us a whole year to learn how to wipe, and flush, and wash our hands, and sit in a circle. So I don't think they truly appreciate some of the levels the children come in on."

One kindergarten teacher suggests that preschool programs should teach more academic skills to accommodate the needs and expectations children will have in kindergarten. Other kindergarten teachers suggested that parent education should be provided to help parents with the shift in expectations from preschool to kindergarten. Some kindergarten teachers view the responsibility for this parent education to lie with the preschool program.

"It would be helpful if some kind of education could be done with [parents] about what kindergarten is going to be like. I think they need to perceive that their relationship with school is going to change."

"It might be useful for the preschool to give [the parents] an overview of what a 5-year-old is going to be like—how the expectations are going to change from preschool to kindergarten, about academics or being a little more independent."

The different realities of the preschool and kindergarten experiences create challenges in the relationships among preschools, kindergartens, and families. For some, these challenges lead to a sense of frustration; for others, a desire to improve the coordination of curricula. As children enter kindergarten, the changes in structure, choices in activities, class size, academic goals, number of daily transitions, and changes in parent involvement require schools and families to address these pronounced differences in order to smooth the transition into school.

Communication Processes

The shift in school expectations affects communication processes between preschool programs and kindergarten, as well as between schools and families. Communication processes can influence expectations as well. Many teachers feel that they lack strong connections with other teachers and programs, and they experience frustration with how information is communicated. Some preschool teachers feel unappreciated by kindergarten teachers. From their perspective, kindergarten teachers are not interested in learning information about incoming children, possibly attributable to kindergarten teachers' concern about potential bias against the children. These preschool teachers express a good deal of frustration in their relationship with kindergarten teachers:

"A lot of our philosophy here in this [preschool] program, I'm extremely frustrated, is not carried over into kindergarten. It's a 1-year thing, and it's gone. You get into sort of the politics of the school and how well the kindergarten staff regards the preschool program. I think we get more negative comments than anything else."

"I asked [kindergarten teachers], 'How are they doing?' and I get one- or two-word answers. So I feel cut off from knowing how well the kids have done. I think that's a critically missing piece between this program and kindergarten. At the end of last year, I told everyone I was available to sit down with them and talk to them about the child that they would get and no one took me up on it. No one. So for me, that's a missing link."

"No one, not one kindergarten teacher has ever sat down in this class to see what our routine is and to see how we play and how much is done through play. So I think there's a really big lack of connections, and I try not to let that be reflected to the parents, or to them, or to the children. I do what I can do in this year, and then hopefully have built a strong enough bridge to move them on and get them really excited that they're visiting their kindergarten teachers."

When the preschool program is housed in the elementary school, communication is seen as more effective. Kindergarten teachers generally view their relationships with preschool teachers as supportive in these situations. The proximity of the preschool classroom to kindergarten classrooms fosters continuity of programs and the various services provided:

"We've got a good communication running between the preschool teacher, the [teaching assistant], and with us. It's like if there's kids that they expect to need to do a child study [on we can] plan [for] those kids and jump right on that versus letting them wait a whole 6–9 months."

"It's nice because if you have a child that, all of a sudden, they're acting up and it's like, 'What's going on?' you can call them and they'll say, 'Well, she did this last year.'"

The proximity of programs sets the groundwork for positive parental attitudes toward the school and positive relationships with teachers:

"The [preschool] program in general helps. A lot of at-risk parents have this experience that their school experience was not a positive one, and because they have the once-a-month family night, have a meal and have a program, I think that helps them have a better attitude about school before they even get to kindergarten. The family trusts the school and the personnel."

In schools where the elementary school is distinct from the preschool program, the connection is viewed as weaker. One preschool principal indicates that communication is lacking between preschool teachers and kindergarten teachers. This is harmful to children because it translates into less continuity from one level to the next:

"I've heard that teachers [say] 'We don't get a chance to hear what goes on in other schools. We don't get a chance to share our ideas that go across schools.' They're very insulated right now."

This principal made efforts to increase the communication between kindergarten and preschool, but she did not think that the levels of communication were sufficient:

"We've had walk-throughs where kindergarten teachers can sign up and go to other schools and see what goes on here at [this school]. And there were also walk-throughs at other elementary schools that teachers could sign up for. Last year, we had a kindergarten teacher, she was a former kindergarten teacher come and talk to us about some of the expectations that kindergarten teachers have. So that helps, but it's so superficial that it's got to move to another level."

In addition to communication regarding children and programs, communication about overall transition practices to enhance children's school entry is influenced by the nature of relationships among school personnel. Children benefit from a mutually shared goal of enhancing children's transitions among everyone involved in the process. If the support exists from the top down, teachers are more inclined to be receptive, which helps to smooth expectations.

Absence of administrative support affects kindergarten teachers' attitudes about transition activities and the family workers' role in implementing these activities. In one case, the principal lacked understanding of the family worker's role and resisted early placement decisions for the preschoolers within his school. Also, preschool administrators work hard to support a sense of community in which families feel comfortable. Because of this, relationships with parents are strongly encouraged, often in ways not evident in kindergartens. Parents are invited to participate and have ongoing contact with school. They are welcomed into the classroom at any time, without making special arrangements. This helps create a greater sense of community for the children, as well. In the preschool teachers' view, kindergarten is less welcoming toward parents. Kindergarten teachers are less likely to request parental input or advice in how to manage problems children may be experiencing. According to these preschool teachers, parents' contact with kindergarten teachers usually occurs when children do something wrong. In preschool, however, these preschool teachers made a concerted effort to keep in constant contact with parents whether children are doing well or are having difficulties:

"I think feedback is key. Feedback to the children and feedback to the parents."

"I worry about the dialogue between school and parents. There's not a lot of dialogue and parents say they would like something back on their children once in a while—a little note. Parents can be scared to ask and sometimes we need to initiate that dialogue. We need to build rapport with parents and say, 'Yeah, come on in. Oh, you have a question

about milk money. That's okay. No question is stupid or little. Let me help.' Sometimes in our professionalism, we put a wall up and people don't see us as real people."

One principal noted that family–school relationships are hierarchical in nature. Families have a limited sense of power in relation to teachers. This perception needs to be addressed:

"You've got to make parents feel like you're not talking down to them, that they're partners with you, that we're all on the same level. We have the same goals, and we all give what we can give. Parent involvement means more than hanging out at school every day. We would like to have you here, but there are different levels to parent involvement. With some parents, it is impossible to come into the building often."

Family workers described the challenges for parents in their relationships with kindergarten. In one particular school, many parents were displeased with the decreased contact with kindergarten teachers, compared with the amount of contact they had with preschool teachers. This led to misunderstandings. One teacher described the situation:

"The misunderstandings possibly drag on a lot longer because there's just not as much communication. The kindergarten teachers are definitely busier, they don't have full time aids, and they're just a little more closed off to parents helping out. They don't have the occasions—we have monthly field trips in [preschool]. So far, the kindergarten teachers have had one field trip all year."

Parents' relationship with school is further challenged by their work schedules. This reality makes it difficult for parents who otherwise would be quite interested in participating:

"They would like to be spending more time in the classroom and because of—it's almost always been because of their work schedule. They're not able to do that. I know that they would really like to spend more time in the classroom. Especially in the beginning of the year, it would have been helpful for their children. So I have heard from parents that teachers are receptive and they're comfortable, but they can't do it because of work."

Some kindergarten teachers express frustration with parents who have difficulty with taking responsibility for their role in their children's education. This creates tension with families.

"We do ask some things. For instance, homework is ignored. For example, I sent home a note for conferences yesterday saying, 'I want to talk with you and I think it's very important, and I hope you feel the same way.' Out of my whole class, not one parent responded."

"You'll say, 'Your mom signed that, you can go get a book,' and he'll say, 'Mommy didn't read that book to me.' So it's an issue of honesty. He learned very quickly that a mom can do this, so he can, too. It sends mixed messages to a child."

"I tell my kids, 'It's your responsibility to keep everything in your folder and to bring it back.' I have to tell them if I know that their parents aren't going to do it because they have to learn and hopefully they will even though their parents don't look at it."

"The parents aren't cooperating right from the start."

Principals also are challenged in effectively connecting with parents. One principal expressed frustration with parents providing adequate structure for their children in preparing for kindergarten:

"Students aren't necessarily getting the rest they need. Sometimes, it's because parents are not as well educated about the importance of a routine, the importance of school. A lot of what we're doing is educating parents, too. Once you decide to have your student in school, you need to take it seriously; even in kindergarten, they need to be here on time. Sometimes the habits are not there. Kids are coming in tired, they're coming in late, and we can't seem to get the parents to understand that they're setting the tone for their life. And it's because they don't value that. That's hard."

Teachers generally value the family worker's role as essential in fostering family–school relationships. By having a family worker available, communication between families and schools is promoted:

"One of the biggest pluses with the preschool and them coming to kindergarten is [the family worker]. She is wonderful in sharing information about the families and talking with families, telling them what they need to know, and continuing to follow up throughout the year."

"[The family worker] has built some relationships with some of these families who might not necessarily feel so great about coming into the school situation and she bridges the gap."

"She really makes herself available. It's not like somebody that we see on occasion. She also makes sure that parents get here for conferences."

Overall, communication among school personnel is made more complicated by the conflicting expectations between preschool and elementary schools. Yet, good communication can help smooth out these differences in expectations at least make them more manageable for children and families. Most personnel value their relationship with families and feel it is important to promote positive communication. The intensity of communication decreases in kindergarten because of multiple constraints and a shift in philosophy. Communication is generally viewed more positively, however, when the preschool program is housed in the elementary school, and it can be facilitated by a family worker who works closely with preschool and kindergarten families.

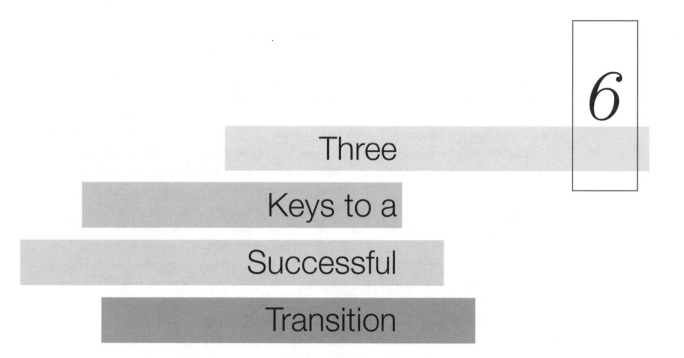

6

Three Keys to a Successful Transition

Collaboration, partnering, and building relationships make more sense during the transition to kindergarten than they do in almost any other time of educating young children. This is a time of change for families, children, and schools in which new expectations, new relationships, and new competencies are formed that can have long-term consequences. For this reason, the efforts to understand the transition to kindergarten and to find ways to enhance transition outcomes for children, families, and schools are important aspects of a community's approach to educating its young citizens. A community can use the efforts described in this volume to further its transition planning. This chapter briefly reflects on lessons learned from the implementation of this approach in a variety of settings, drawing implications for future work. Three conclusions stand out—the centrality of collaboration and relationships, the importance of a conceptual model that all stakeholders can use as a guide, and the value of working through community-guided efforts for long-term gains.

COLLABORATION AND RELATIONSHIPS

It is clear that good transition planning and implementation involves collaboration and relationships, and this is a two-way street, involving both giving and receiving. Collaboration is a central part of the approach we recommend. It is central to our conceptualization of the transition process. It is the key to good transition planning and implementation. Effective relationships are key outcomes of helpful transition practices and policies. Thus, we focus on building partnerships and relationships as the key to enhancing transition outcomes.

Collaboration and partnerships enable new ideas to have roots in local realities (Denner, Cooper, Lopez, & Dunbar, 1999). It is impossible for even the best-designed intervention or reform efforts to be adequately implemented in communities and schools when reformers and constituents are not working as partners. Turnbull (1998) applied a collaborative model both in terms of family–school and family–researcher cooperation that was similar to our approach. In this model, families and educators played equal roles in the design of initiatives. The literature points to a number of key elements of collaboration (Carnine, 1997; Denner et al., 1999; Groark & McCall, 1996), including the need for explicit goals among all of the participants. Common goals are best developed in the context of articulating a shared mission that benefits all of the participants, and relationships among collaborators can then be developed with a sense of trust and mutual respect.

Our approach views the quality of the collaborative process and the relationships among the participants as *the* central criterion by which to evaluate our day-to-day efforts and the longer-term results of the transition plan. To be successful, this often involves giving up certain views or priorities about what might be the best practice or the key issue involved in a certain situation and adopting a new or different perspective offered by another collaborator. This is not easy; yet over time, it helps develop a sense of mutuality and trust that makes change easier.

A CONCEPTUAL MODEL AS A GUIDE

We started with a conceptual model of the transition process that was based on decades of research and practice in early childhood and elementary education, using a lens of systems theory (Bronfenbrenner & Morris, 1997; Pianta & Walsh, 1996; Rimm-Kaufman & Pianta, 1999). This approach emphasizes relationships among an array of contexts and over time as the key engine of developmental growth and change. In this view, adjustment in the transition to school is a product of relationships among a wide array of contexts and people, including the child, his or her family, schools and teachers, peers, and the wider community. Interactions among these contexts and people can be important sources of support that foster early school success, particularly for children for whom transition to school may be a challenge.

A key aspect of the success of this approach to transition has always been reliance on this conceptual model as a guide for local planning and implementation efforts. Just as collaboration and relationships serve as criteria for judging whether the process of transition planning and implementation is going well, the conceptual model serves as a guide for generating ideas about the concrete practices and policies that need to be addressed in a transition plan. On many occasions, we have observed collaborators using the conceptual model as a tool for deciding whether the transition practices in their community are comprehensive or adequate enough. We have observed collaborative teams using the model as a means of brainstorming about what could be done in their community. Having a common idea about the transition process itself and a vision for what it could be was key to successful collaboration and implementation.

COMMUNITY-GUIDED EFFORTS

Finally, a key conclusion drawn from our experiences is that every family's transition needs are different and that an inflexible program is bound to be a failure from the outset. This is particularly true for families whose lives are very complex—who face challenges in housing and income, schooling, personal resources, and social stresses. We designed a menu-based approach to implementing good transition practices. This approach directs the creation of open-ended transition plans that describe a variety of practices designed to enhance relationships among children, peers, families, and schools. These practices follow from a common model of transition and reflect key principles and values that had been embraced by the collaborators. Thus, these practices focus on relationships among key contexts and people, they emphasize the importance of continuity over time starting well before entry into kindergarten, and they embrace the principle that interactions be based on mutual respect and support for the child. All of these decisions are local decisions made by the collaborators themselves in response to the perceived needs of the constituents they serve (families and educators) in that community. In the end, an emphasis on community-guided efforts enables this approach to transition planning to be implemented in a variety of school settings, each with its own unique organizational structure and constraints

These three features—a priority on collaboration and relationships, adopting a common conceptual model or guide, and having local communities and individuals' needs and goals as central drivers of change—are key aspects of this process that will lead to its taking roots in a community or school and working over time to produce change consistent with the overall mission or goals. The best and most successful transition planning and implementation efforts are those owned by the community's schools, teachers, and families. We hope you find this book and the approach it describes useful in your attempts to assist children and families during this important period of life. Your efforts can go a long way toward helping children start school on the right foot!

Appendix

This appendix contains blank examples of forms that transition teams can use. These forms are based on those used in the Kindergarten Transition Project. Purchasers of this book are welcome to photocopy and use these forms in their transition programs if the forms are appropriate to the needs of the transition teams, parents, and children. If they are not, readers are encouraged to create their own forms, using these examples as guidelines.

Transition Interview

I'd like to talk to you about children's transitions into kindergarten and your experiences with the kindergarten transition process.

1. First, think about children who may be at risk and children who have had successful transitions into kindergarten. When this transition goes smoothly, what factors are in place that make the process go well? *[For preschool teachers, just refer to children whom they have taught. Follow up with these questions if all issues are not addressed.]*

   - What characteristics of the child and the family help this process go well?

   - What characteristics of the preschool program help foster the transition into school?

   - What characteristics of the kindergarten program help this process move smoothly? Are there particular program characteristics that help?

   - Are there other contributing factors?

2. Are children's transitions into kindergarten a problem at your school? If so, in what ways?

3. What are the challenges in helping children make the transition to kindergarten in your school? Are there any particular barriers?

4. Are there other things that schools could do to help children become familiar with school?

5. Now, I'd like to ask you about your impressions of the transition process and your experiences. In what aspects of the process did you participate? For example, did you participate in transition activities for preschoolers entering kindergarten or other activities to enhance relationships for children and families as they entered kindergarten?

   - What went well?

   - What changes might you make?

6. Is there anything more you wish to share about children's transition into kindergarten?

Figure A1. An example of a Transition Interview. Transition coordinators use this form to interview school and community participants about the transition process.

Successful Kindergarten Transition: Your Guide to Connecting Children, Families, and Schools
by Robert C. Pianta, Ph.D., and Marcia Kraft-Sayre, L.C.S.W. © 2003 Paul H. Brookes Publishing Co., Inc.

Transition Practices Brainstorming Guide

Transition practice	Connections fostered	Priority	Who	When	Barriers and solutions	Linkages and notes

Figure A2. An example of a Transition Practices Brainstorming Guide.

Successful Kindergarten Transition: Your Guide to Connecting Children, Families, and Schools by Robert C. Pianta, Ph.D., and Marcia Kraft-Sayre, L.C.S.W. © 2003 Paul H. Brookes Publishing Co., Inc.

Transition Timeline Worksheet

Month	Date to be initiated	Activity	Who's in charge	Special needs	Carryover?

Figure A3. An example of a Transition Timeline Worksheet.

Successful Kindergarten Transition: Your Guide to Connecting Children, Families, and Schools
by Robert C. Pianta, Ph.D., and Marcia Kraft-Sayre, L.C.S.W. © 2003 Paul H. Brookes Publishing Co., Inc.

93

Checklist for Community Transition Steering Committees

Brainstorm

☐ Address all types of connections.

☐ Seek input from family members, school staff members, and communities members who will be affected by the success of our transition program.

☐ Identify and resolve barriers.

Allocate resources

☐ Give teachers the flexibility and compensation to fulfill their transition role.

☐ Hire substitutes, arrange class coverage, or stagger the start of school for kindergartners so that teachers can do home visits.

☐ Consider providing child care for parents attending school functions.

☐ Solicit feedback from teachers about what their needs are during transition.

Create realistic timelines

☐ Revise the timelines according to anticipated barriers.

☐ Use in-service meetings to orient teachers and parents to the program's goals.

Involve parents

☐ Alert parents of meetings in advance and schedule meetings so that most parents can attend.

☐ Reach out to parents so that they feel welcome.

☐ Ask parents about the issues that concern them.

☐ Solicit feedback from parents about their needs are during transition.

Identify evaluation procedures

☐ Choose evaluation measures.

☐ Clarify a timeline for collecting feedback.

☐ Identify who is responsible for collecting feedback.

☐ Seek feedback from all involved in the transition process.

Figure A4. An example of a Checklist for Community Transition Steering Committees.

Checklist for Transition Coordinators

Family connections

☐ Make contact in first 2 weeks

☐ Assess family needs and link up with services

☐ Encourage parents to foster peer connections

☐ Send home newsletters

☐ Schedule regular meetings

☐ Encourage parents to foster peer contact

☐ Help organize back-to-school nights and transition orientations

☐ Encourage home-learning activities

Peer connections

☐ Help teachers establish peer connections at school

☐ Introduce each child to the kindergarten teacher

☐ Help kindergarten generate class lists that pair friendly peers

School connections

☐ Foster inter-school discussions about programs and class-room practices

☐ Encourage events cosponsored by the preschool and the kindergarten

☐ Initiate meetings between preschool and kindergarten teachers about children

Community connections

☐ Help clarify community needs and expectations regarding schools and transition

☐ Meet regularly with the transition team

Figure A5. An example of a Checklist for Transition Coordinators.

Successful Kindergarten Transition: Your Guide to Connecting Children, Families, and Schools by Robert C. Pianta, Ph.D., and Marcia Kraft-Sayre, L.C.S.W. © 2003 Paul H. Brookes Publishing Co., Inc.

Checklist for Preschool Teachers

Family connections

☐ Make contact in first 2 weeks
☐ Encourage participation
☐ Participate in regular meetings with parents
☐ Attend back-to-school nights and transition orientations
☐ Provide home-learning activities

Peer connections

☐ Promote peer connections at school
☐ Encourage parents to promote peer connections outside of school

School connections

☐ Invite kindergarten staff to visit preschool
☐ Discuss expectations for transition with kindergarten teachers
☐ Discuss particular children with kindergarten staff
☐ Practice kindergarten rituals
☐ Make contact with former students

Community connections

☐ Stay apprised on the transition team's goals and plans
☐ Participate in meetings about transition

Checklist for Kindergarten Teachers

Family connections

☐ Make contact in first 2 weeks
☐ Encourage participation
☐ Participate in regular meetings with parents
☐ Attend back-to-school nights and transition orientations

Peer connections

☐ Promote peer connections at school
☐ Encourage parents to promote peer connections outside of school

School connections

☐ Invite preschoolers to visit
☐ Discuss expectations for transition with preschool teachers
☐ Discuss particular children with preschool staff
☐ Incorporate preschool rituals
☐ Visit the preschool classroom
☐ Encourage contact with the preschool teacher

Community connections

☐ Stay apprised of the transition team's goals and plans
☐ Participate in meetings about transition

Checklist for Principals

Family connections

☐ Encourage participation
☐ Participate in regular meetings with parents
☐ Schedule and coordinate transition activities

Peer connections

☐ Support teachers in promoting peer connections at school
☐ Encourage parents to promote peer connections outside of school

School connections

☐ Support collaboration between programs
☐ Discuss expectations for transition with kindergarten and preschool teachers
☐ Discuss particular children with kindergarten and preschool staff

Community connections

☐ Help shape the transition goals and plans
☐ Work with the school district to create transition-supportive policy
☐ Think creatively about resource allocation to support teachers
☐ Seek community agencies' support of transition goals and activities
☐ Participate in meetings about transition

Figure A6. A sample Checklist for Preschool Teachers. **Figure A7.** A sample Checklist for Kindergarten Teachers. **Figure A8.** A sample Checklist for Principals.

Successful Kindergarten Transition: Your Guide to Connecting Children, Families, and Schools by Robert C. Pianta, Ph.D., and Marcia Kraft-Sayre, L.C.S.W. © 2003 Paul H. Brookes Publishing Co., Inc.

Kindergarten Transition Contact Log

Directions: This form is for documenting contacts with elementary school personnel or family members of children experiencing kindergarten transition. Indicate the date, the person with whom you had contact, the setting, the topics discussed, and your general impressions of the meeting.

Date	Name/initials	Person with whom you had contact	Type/Setting	Topics discussed	General impressions

Figure A9. An example of a Kindergarten Transition Contact Log.

Successful Kindergarten Transition: Your Guide to Connecting Children, Families, and Schools by Robert C. Pianta, Ph.D., and Marcia Kraft-Sayre, L.C.S.W. © 2003 Paul H. Brookes Publishing Co., Inc.

96

Instructions for Kindergarten Transition Menu Checklist

Please complete the menu checklist at the end of each week to document transition activities. For every child listed, check the box or boxes that correspond with activities you have used to promote connections. Check as many boxes as apply for each activity. (The Transition Activities Menu in *Successful Kindergarten Transition: Your Guide to Connecting Children, Families, and Schools* describes the types of activities in detail.)

Also, please describe your impressions of the transition activities you are implementing, including the nature of each specific activity, your thoughts on its effectiveness, what contributed to its success, and what may have impeded its implementation. You may document this information on the back of the checklist or keep a separate running log.

FAMILY–SCHOOL ACTIVITIES

- Meetings about transition issues
  - Meeting at preschool with the kindergarten teachers and/or parents of kindergartners
  - Meeting at the elementary school before the onset of kindergarten
- A family, the preschool teacher, and the kindergarten teacher meeting to share information about a child
- Meetings to orient parents to programs after school starts

CHILD–SCHOOL CONTACT

- Contact between preschool and kindergarten
  - A preschooler's connection with the kindergarten teacher
  - A preschooler's connection with the elementary school for special school functions
  - A preschooler's practice of kindergarten activities
  - Kindergarten activities incorporated from preschool
  - The preschool teacher's visits to former students in their kindergarten class

PRESCHOOL PEER CONTACT

- Peer connections outside of school
- Peer connections with nonclassmate peers who will be in the same kindergarten class
- Group-based peer connections (activity-based social skills groups)
- Peer connections within the class are assumed and do not need to be checked

KINDERGARTEN PEER CONTACT

- Preschool peer connections with kindergarten peers
  - Kindergartners visit preschool
  - Preschoolers visit kindergarten class
  - Summer school inclusion of rising kindergartners

COMMUNITY CONTACT

- Contact with other schools
- Inter-school collaboration about programs and classroom practices
  - School policy coordination
  - Classroom practices discussion
- Inter-school connection concerning a specific child
- Contact with agencies
- Connections with community agencies

DESCRIPTION OF ACTIVITY

Describe the transition activity being noted. Also, describe practices you have used that are not included elsewhere. Include connection-building activities you are aware of but have not directly initiated. For example, mention reports of peers playing with one another outside of school or families connecting with one another. Your impressions of the effectiveness of activities can also be highlighted.

Figure A10. Instructions for using the sample Kindergarten Transition Menu Checklist.

Successful Kindergarten Transition: Your Guide to Connecting Children, Families, and Schools
by Robert C. Pianta, Ph.D., and Marcia Kraft-Sayre, L.C.S.W. © 2003 Paul H. Brookes Publishing Co., Inc.

Kindergarten Transition Menu Checklist

Directions: Check as many boxes as apply.

Week of _____

Student	Family–school activities	Child–school contact	Preschool peer contact	Kindergarten peer contact	Community contact	Description of activity

Figure A11. An example of a Kindergarten Transition Menu Checklist.

Successful Kindergarten Transition: Your Guide to Connecting Children, Families, and Schools
by Robert C. Pianta, Ph.D., and Marcia Kraft-Sayre, L.C.S.W. © 2003 Paul H. Brookes Publishing Co., Inc.

Kindergarten Transition Parent Interview—Preschool (page 1)

Interviewer: _____   Date: _____

Location of interview (e.g., family home): _____

Person interviewed (e.g., mother, grandparent): _____

Other family members present: _____

Directions: Use the following text as a guide to help families explore their experiences in the fall, winter, and spring of preschool. The intent is to engage the family member in a conversation about school, following up on themes that arise. These are some components of an interview. Other questions may be added. For example, the parent may be asked about family stresses, coping, and their social support network. Ideally, responses should be recorded using an audiotape recorder so that the conversation flows more smoothly. If the family member feels uncomfortable being audiotaped, write his or her answers on separate pieces of paper. Further directions appear in brackets in italic print.

We are interested in learning about children's and families' experiences in preschool. Today, I am interested in talking with you about your child's experiences in preschool this year. I would like to know how these experiences may be similar and how they are different. All of your comments will be kept confidential. Do you have any questions before we begin? *[Pause for any questions.]*

YOUR CHILD'S EXPERIENCES AT SCHOOL

1. First, I'd like to talk to you about your child's experiences in school. Tell me how *[child's name]* is doing in school this year. *[Ask the family member to tell you more. Use the following prompts to encourage further discussion. You do not need to ask all of the questions.]*

   - What types of things are he or she learning?
   - What does he or she like to do in school? *[Suggest, if necessary, circle time, center time, playground time, reading, story time, and so forth.]*
   - What activities does he or she not like to do?
   - Tell me about your child's progress this year. What are you particularly pleased with? What do you have concerns about?

2. Tell me about your child's behavior at school this year.

   - How well does your child get along with classmates?
   - How does he or she get along with kids outside of school?
   - How well does he or she get along with his or her teacher?

3. Tell me about your involvement this year at school.

4. What's your relationship with your child's teacher like?

PEER CONTACT

1. Now, I'd like to ask you about your child's contact with other children. Outside of school, what kind of things does your child do with other children? *[If necessary, suggest playing with other children in the neighborhood, attending after-school programs, playing with sibling or other relatives, and so forth.]*

2. Do any of the children your child plays with go to preschool with him or her? Which activities?

(continued)

Figure A12.   An example of a Kindergarten Transition Parent Interview–Preschool.

Successful Kindergarten Transition: Your Guide to Connecting Children, Families, and Schools
by Robert C. Pianta, Ph.D., and Marcia Kraft-Sayre, L.C.S.W. © 2003 Paul H. Brookes Publishing Co., Inc.

Kindergarten Transition Parent Interview—Preschool (page 2)

YOUR CHILD'S ACTIVITIES AT HOME

1. Now I'd like to ask you about your child's activities and behavior at home. What kinds of activities do you and your child enjoy together?
   - What things do you like to do with your child to help him or her learn? [*If necessary, suggest reading, talking about numbers or letters, singing songs, and so forth.*]
2. Tell me about your child's behavior at home this year.
   - When your child is frustrated or upset, what does he or she do? How do you handle this?

YOUR ACTIVITIES WITH THE SCHOOL

Now I'd like to ask you about things you've been involved with at the school. Parents help at school in different ways, depending on their situations. What kinds of activities have you been involved with at your child's school this year? [*First, allow the parent to answer freely, then prompt for those activities not mentioned. Follow up on the frequency for activities mentioned.*]

Activity	Never	1–2 times	3 or more times
1. Contacted the child's teacher through notes			
2. Talked with the child's teacher by telephone or in person			
3. Talked with other parents from the child's school			
4. Talked with the school director or principal this year			
5. Attended parent–teacher conferences			
6. Prepared and sent in food or materials for special events or holidays (e.g., class activity, Valentine's Day)			
7. Attended special schoolwide events for children and families (e.g., family literacy activities, book fairs)			
8. Volunteered or helped out in the classroom			
9. Helped with field trips or other special events			
10. Attended a meeting of the parent–teacher organization			
11. Visited with the teacher or other school staff in the home			
12. Other (Please specify.)			

FAMILY INFORMATION

1. I'd like to ask you a few questions about your family. Who lives at home with your child? Please tell me their relationship with your child and their ages (e.g., 10-year-old sister).
2. Are you currently employed? If so, what type of work do you do? On average, how many hours do you work per week?
3. Are there adults living in the house? If so, do they work? What kind of work? What hours do they work?

Kindergarten Transition Parent Interview—Kindergarten (page 1)

Interviewer: _____ Date: _____

Location of interview (e.g., family home): _____

Person interviewed (e.g., mother, grandparent): _____

Other family members present: _____

Directions: Use the following text as a guide to help families explore their experiences in the fall, winter, and spring of kindergarten. The intent is to engage the family member in a conversation about school, following up on themes that arise. These are some components of an interview. Other questions may be added. Ideally, responses should be recorded using an audiotape recorder so that the conversation flows more smoothly. If the family member feels uncomfortable being audiotaped, write his or her answers on separate pieces of paper. Further directions appear in brackets in italic print.

As you know from our previous interviews, we are interested in learning about children's and families' experiences in kindergarten. Today, I am interested in talking with you more generally about his or her experiences, both in preschool and in kindergarten this year. I would like to know how these experiences may be similar and how they are different. As before, all of your answers will be kept confidential. Do you have any questions before we begin? *[Pause for any questions.]*

YOUR CHILD'S EXPERIENCES AT SCHOOL

1. First, I'd like to talk to you about your child's experiences in school. Tell me how *[child's name]* is doing in school this year and how this compares with last year. *[Ask the family member to tell you more. Use the following prompts to encourage further discussion. you do not need to ask all of the questions.]*

   - What types of things are he or she learning? How do these things compare with what he or she was doing last year? What seems to be the same about what he or she was doing last year? What seems different?
   - What does he or she like to do in school? *[Suggest, if necessary, writing, reading, math, center time, playground time, and so forth.]* How does this compare with pre-school?
   - What activities does he or she not like to do?
   - Tell me about your child's progress this year. What are you particularly pleased with? What do you have concerns about?

2. Tell me about your child's behavior at school this year. Is this a change from last year? If so, in what way?

   - How well does your child get along with classmates?
   - How does he or she get along with kids outside of school?
   - How well does he or she get along with his or her teacher?
   - Do teachers expect similar behavior from your child in kindergarten as in preschool? Are there differences in, for example, how strict or structured they are?

3. Tell me about your involvement this year at school. How does it compare with last year?

4. What's your relationship with your child's teacher like?

(continued)

Figure A13. An example of a Kindergarten Transition Parent Interview–Kindergarten

Successful Kindergarten Transition: Your Guide to Connecting Children, Families, and Schools
by Robert C. Pianta, Ph.D., and Marcia Kraft-Sayre, L.C.S.W. © 2003 Paul H. Brookes Publishing Co., Inc.

Kindergarten Transition Parent Interview—Kindergarten (page 2)

PEER CONTACT

1. Now, I'd like to ask you about your child's contact with other children. Outside of school, what kind of things does your child do with other children? *[If necessary, suggest playing with other children in the neighborhood; attending after-school programs; playing with siblings, cousins, or other relatives; attending religious functions; and so forth.]*

2. Do any of the children involved in these activities with your child go to kindergarten with him or her? Which activities?

YOUR CHILD'S ACTIVITIES AT HOME

1. Now I'd like to ask you about your child's activities and behavior at home. What kinds of activities do you and your child enjoy together?
   - What things do you like to do with your child to help him or her learn? *[If necessary, suggest reading, talking about numbers or letters, singing songs, and so forth.]*

2. Tell me about your child's behavior at home this year. How does this compare with his or her behavior at school?
   - When your child is frustrated or upset, what does he or she do? How do you handle this?

REFLECTIONS ON THE TRANSITION TO KINDERGARTEN

Now I'd like to ask you some questions about your child's experience with going to kindergarten. I'm interested in how he or she got to know kindergarten before it started and what this has been like for him or her and for you.

1. First, how has the experience of going into kindergarten been for your child? *[Allow time for a response and then follow up with the next question.]* In general, would you say it's been very good, fairly good, just okay, or neutral? Do you have some concerns? Do you have many concerns?

2. What has gone well for your child? *[Encourage elaboration, and check all areas that apply.]*

   _____ Learning   _____ Social

   _____ Other   _____ None

3. What has been hard for him or her? What has not gone well for your child? *[Encourage elaboration, and check all areas that apply.]*

   _____ Learning   _____ Social

   _____ Other   _____ None

4. What has gone well for you?

5. What has been hard for you?

REFLECTIONS ON THE TRANSITION TO KINDERGARTEN *(cont.)*

6. The way families help their children learn about kindergarten depends, in part, on how familiar they and their children already are with the school. Have you or your child had experience with *[name of school]* before this year? If yes, in what ways? *[Check all that apply.]*

    _____ Your child attended preschool at the same school last year.

    _____ You have another child who attended the same school.

    _____ You attended the same school.

    _____ Another family member attended the same school. If so, state the relationship.

    _____ Other. (Please state how.)

7. I'd like you to remember the time your child went to preschool. What kind of things did you do with *[name of school]* to help your child learn about kindergarten? *[First, allow the family member to answer freely. If other activities are mentioned, add them under "Other." Once the parent responds, ask about the remaining activities.]*

School activity	Yes	No
1. Visited kindergarten classroom in the spring		
2. Attended a spring kindergarten orientation		
3. Attended kindergarten registration		
4. Attended a summer activity at the elementary school		
5. Visited the kindergarten classroom before school started during the school's open house night		
6. Participated in kindergarten screening		
7. Attended "Back to School Night"		
8. Met the child's kindergarten teacher		
9. Met the school principal		
10. Got a tour of the school		
11. Talked to parents of the child's classmates		
12. Talked with the child's preschool teacher or transition coordinator about transition issues		
13. Received a letter or written information from the school		
14. Received a telephone call from the child's kindergarten teacher		
15. Had a home visit from the child's kindergarten teacher		
16. Other (Please specify.)		

(continued)

Figure A13. *(continued)*

Kindergarten Transition Parent Interview—Kindergarten (page 4)

REFLECTIONS ON THE TRANSITION TO KINDERGARTEN *(cont.)*

8. Of these activities, which three have been most useful? *[Write down the number of the item identified. If fewer than three are identified, ask about the usefulness of the activities mentioned.]*

9. What kinds of things could the school do to help make your child more comfortable in kindergarten?

10. What kinds of things could the school do to help make you more comfortable?

PREPARING FOR KINDERGARTEN

In addition to activities at schools, families often do activities on their own to get their child ready for kindergarten. What kinds of activities did you do during the summer to get your child ready for school? *[Allow the family member to respond freely. After the family member responds, use the prompts if necessary for the remaining activities.]* There are other things that parents sometimes do. It is not expected that parents do all of these things. The activities that a family does depend on a number of factors, such as whether a child has brothers or sisters who attend the same school. Knowing this, did you do any other following activities?

Activity	Yes	No
1. Did you read parents' magazines or books about starting kindergarten?		
2. Did you read stories to your child about starting kindergarten?		
3. Did you take your child to play on the school playground?		
4. Did you talk with other parents of children from your child's school?		
5. Did you talk with family members or friends who have school-age children?		
6. Did you teach your child his or her address?		
7. Did you teach your child his or her telephone number?		
8. Did you teach your child to tie his or her shoes?		
9. Did you discuss what will happen on the first day of school with your child?		
10. Did you discuss meeting the new teacher with your child?		
11. Did you discuss meeting new classmates with your child?		
12. Did you discuss how to behave with your child?		
13. Did you discuss the kinds of kindergarten work with your child?		
14. Did you practice daily routines of getting ready for school (e.g., bed-time, morning schedule)?		
15. Other (Please specify.)		

Successful Kindergarten Transition: Your Guide to Connecting Children, Families, and Schools
by Robert C. Pianta, Ph.D., and Marcia Kraft-Sayre, L.C.S.W. © 2003 Paul H. Brookes Publishing Co., Inc.

Kindergarten Transition Parent Interview—Kindergarten (page 5)

YOUR ACTIVITIES WITH THE SCHOOL

Now I'd like to ask you about things you've been involved with at the school. Parents help at school in different ways, depending on their situations. What kinds of activities have you been involved with at your child's school this year? *[First, allow the parent to answer freely, then prompt for those activities not mentioned. Follow up on the frequency for activities mentioned.]*

Activity	Never	1–2 times	3 or more times
1. Helped the child with homework			
2. Contacted the child's teacher through notes			
3. Talked with the child's teacher by telephone or in person			
4. Talked with other parents from the child's school			
5. Talked with the school principal this year			
6. Attended parent–teacher conferences			
7. Prepared and sent in food or materials for special events or holidays (e.g., class activity, Valentine's Day)			
8. Attended special schoolwide events for children and families (e.g., family literacy activities, book fairs)			
9. Volunteered or helped out in the classroom			
10. Helped with field trips or other special events			
11. Attended a meeting of the parent–teacher organization			
12. Visited with the teacher or other school staff in the home			
13. Other (Please specify.)			

FAMILY INFORMATION

1. I'd like to ask you a few questions to update the general information about your family. Who lives at home with your child? Please tell me their relationship with your child and their ages (e.g., 10-year-old sister). Is this a change from 6 months ago?

2. Are you currently employed? If so, what type of work do you do? On average, how many hours do you work per week? Is this a change from 6 months ago?

3. Are there adults living in the house? If so, do they work? What kind of work? What hours do they work?

4. Have you moved in the last 6 months?

Thank you for sharing information with me today about your family. I appreciate your time.

Successful Kindergarten Transition: Your Guide to Connecting Children, Families, and Schools by Robert C. Pianta, Ph.D., and Marcia Kraft-Sayre, L.C.S.W. © 2003 Paul H. Brookes Publishing Co., Inc.

Transition Activities Questionnaire for Preschool Teachers (page 1)

Name: _____

The following activities relate to helping children make the transition into kindergarten. For each activity, please indicate whether you participated in the activity during this school year with current preschool children. If you participated, please indicate whether you found the activity to be very useful for children and families, somewhat useful, or not useful, by checking the appropriate box.

Transition activity	Participated?	Very useful	Somewhat useful	Not useful
1. Preschool children visited a kindergarten classroom.				
2. Preschool children visited the specific kindergarten class they are anticipated to attend next year.				
3. I visited the kindergarten classroom.				
4. A kindergarten teacher visited my preschool classroom.				
5. Elementary school children visited my preschool classroom.				
6. Preschool children attended a spring orientation about kindergarten.				
7. Parents of preschool children attended an orientation about kindergarten.				
8. Preschool children participated in an elementary schoolwide activity (e.g., assemblies, spring programs).				
9. I had an individual meeting with parent(s) of a preschool child about kindergarten issues.				
10. I shared written records of children's preschool experience and status with elementary school personnel.				
11. I met with kindergarten teachers about the curriculum.				
12. I contacted kindergarten teachers about specific children.				
13. Other activities (Please specify.)				

Figure A14. An example of a Transition Activities Questionnaire for Preschool Teachers.

Successful Kindergarten Transition: Your Guide to Connecting Children, Families, and Schools
by Robert C. Pianta, Ph.D., and Marcia Kraft-Sayre, L.C.S.W. © 2003 Paul H. Brookes Publishing Co., Inc.

Transition Activities Questionnaire for Preschool Teachers (page 2)

1. What has been the most useful transition activity for the children? Why?

_____

_____

_____

_____

2. What has been the least useful transition activity for the children? Why?

_____

_____

_____

_____

3. Are there other activities that you would like to see offered to families to prepare children for kindergarten? If so, list them here.

_____

_____

_____

_____

4. What are your goals with activities to help children make the transition from preschool to kindergarten?

_____

_____

_____

_____

5. Please share any thoughts you may have about transition activities.

_____

_____

_____

_____

Successful Kindergarten Transition: Your Guide to Connecting Children, Families, and Schools
by Robert C. Pianta, Ph.D., and Marcia Kraft-Sayre, L.C.S.W. © 2003 Paul H. Brookes Publishing Co., Inc.

Transition Activities Questionnaire for Kindergarten Teachers (page 1)

Name: _____

The following activities relate to helping children make the transition into kindergarten. For each activity, please indicate whether you participated in the activity during this school year with current preschool children. If you participated, please indicate whether you found the activity to be very useful for children and families, somewhat useful, or not useful, by checking the appropriate box.

Transition activity	Participated?	Very useful	Somewhat useful	Not useful
1. Preschool children visited my kindergarten classroom.				
2. Preschool children whom I expect to teach next year visited my kindergarten classroom.				
3. I visited the preschool program.				
4. A preschool teacher visited my kindergarten classroom.				
5. Elementary school children visited the preschool program.				
6. Preschool children attended a spring orientation about kindergarten.				
7. Parents of preschool children attended an orientation about kindergarten.				
8. I met with a preschool child who will be attending my school.				
9. I met with the family of a preschool child who will be attending my school.				
10. Preschool children participated in an elementary schoolwide activity (e.g., assemblies, spring programs).				
11. I read the written records of children's preschool experience and status.				
12. I contacted preschool teachers about individual children.				
13. I met with preschool teachers about the curriculum				
14. I participated in kindergarten registration for my school.				
13. Other activities (Please specify.)				

Figure A15. An example of a Transition Activities Questionnaire for Kindergarten Teachers.

Successful Kindergarten Transition: Your Guide to Connecting Children, Families, and Schools by Robert C. Pianta, Ph.D., and Marcia Kraft-Sayre, L.C.S.W. © 2003 Paul H. Brookes Publishing Co., Inc.

Transition Activities Questionnaire for Kindergarten Teachers (page 2)

1. What has been the most useful transition activity for the children? Why?

   _____

   _____

   _____

   _____

2. What has been the least useful transition activity for the children? Why?

   _____

   _____

   _____

   _____

3. Are there other activities that you would like to see offered to families to prepare children for kindergarten? If so, list them here.

   _____

   _____

   _____

   _____

4. What are your goals with activities to help children make the transition from preschool to kindergarten?

   _____

   _____

   _____

   _____

5. Please share any thoughts you may have about transition activities.

   _____

   _____

   _____

   _____

Successful Kindergarten Transition: Your Guide to Connecting Children, Families, and Schools
by Robert C. Pianta, Ph.D., and Marcia Kraft-Sayre, L.C.S.W. © 2003 Paul H. Brookes Publishing Co., Inc.

Transition Activities Questionnaire for Transition Coordinators (page 1)

Name: _____

The following activities relate to helping children make the transition into kindergarten. For each activity, please indicate whether you participated in the activity during this school year with current preschool children. If you participated, please indicate whether you found the activity to be very useful for children and families, somewhat useful, or not useful, by checking the appropriate box.

Transition activity	Participated?	Very useful	Somewhat useful	Not useful
1. Preschool children visited a kindergarten classroom.				
2. Preschool children visited the specific kindergarten classroom they are anticipated to attend next year.				
3. I visited a kindergarten classroom.				
4. The preschool teacher visited a kindergarten classroom.				
5. A kindergarten teacher visited the preschool program.				
6. Elementary school children visited the preschool program.				
7. Preschool children attended a spring orientation about kindergarten.				
8. Parents of preschool children attended an orientation about kindergarten.				
9. Preschool children participated in an elementary schoolwide activity (e.g., assemblies, spring programs).				
10. I met with the family of a preschool child about transition issues.				
11. I shared the written records of children's preschool experience and status with elementary school personnel.				
12. I contacted kindergarten teachers about individual children.				
13. Other activities (Please specify.)				

Figure A16. An example of a Transition Activities Questionnaire for Transition Coordinators.

Successful Kindergarten Transition: Your Guide to Connecting Children, Families, and Schools
by Robert C. Pianta, Ph.D., and Marcia Kraft-Sayre, L.C.S.W. © 2003 Paul H. Brookes Publishing Co., Inc.

Transition Activities Questionnaire for Transition Coordinators (page 2)

1. What has been the most useful transition activity for the children? Why?

_____

_____

_____

_____

2. What has been the least useful transition activity for the children? Why?

_____

_____

_____

_____

3. Are there other activities that you would like to see offered to families to prepare children for kindergarten? If so, list them here.

_____

_____

_____

_____

4. What are your goals with activities to help children make the transition from preschool to kindergarten?

_____

_____

_____

_____

5. Please share any thoughts you may have about transition activities.

_____

_____

_____

_____

Successful Kindergarten Transition: Your Guide to Connecting Children, Families, and Schools
by Robert C. Pianta, Ph.D., and Marcia Kraft-Sayre, L.C.S.W. © 2003 Paul H. Brookes Publishing Co., Inc.

Transition Activities Questionnaire for Principals (page 1)

Name: _____

The following activities relate to helping children make the transition into kindergarten. For each activity, please indicate whether you participated in the activity during this school year with current preschool children. If you participated, please indicate whether you found the activity to be very useful for children and families, somewhat useful, or not useful, by checking the appropriate box.

Transition activity	Participated?	Very useful	Somewhat useful	Not useful
1. Preschool children visited a kindergarten classroom.				
2. Preschool children visited the specific kindergarten classroom they will attend next year.				
3. The preschool teacher visited a kindergarten classroom.				
4. A kindergarten teacher visited the preschool program.				
5. Elementary school children visited the preschool program.				
6. Preschool children attended a spring orientation about kindergarten.				
7. Parents of preschool children attended an orientation about kindergarten.				
8. Preschool children who will be attending my school met their kindergarten teacher.				
9. The kindergarten teacher met with the family of a preschool child who will be attending my school.				
10. Preschool children participated in an elementary schoolwide activity (e.g., assemblies, spring programs).				
11. Elementary school personnel read the written records of children's preschool experience and status.				
12. Kindergarten and preschool teachers had a meeting about the curriculum.				
13. The kindergarten teacher and preschool teacher had a meeting about specific children.				
14. Other activities (Please specify.)				

Figure A17. An example of a Transition Activities Questionnaire for Principals.

Successful Kindergarten Transition: Your Guide to Connecting Children, Families, and Schools
by Robert C. Pianta, Ph.D., and Marcia Kraft-Sayre, L.C.S.W. © 2003 Paul H. Brookes Publishing Co., Inc.

Transition Activities Questionnaire for Principals (page 2)

1. What has been the most useful transition activity for the children? Why?

_____

_____

_____

_____

2. What has been the least useful transition activity for the children? Why?

_____

_____

_____

_____

3. Are there other activities that you would like to see offered to families to prepare children for kindergarten? If so, list them here.

_____

_____

_____

_____

4. What are your goals, as a principal, with activities to help children make the transition from preschool to kindergarten?

_____

_____

_____

_____

5. Please share any thoughts you may have about transition activities.

_____

_____

_____

_____

Transition Activities Questionnaire for Parents

Name: _____

The following activities relate to learning about kindergarten. For each activity, please indicate whether you or your child participated in the activity during the school year. If yes, please indicate whether you found the activity to be very useful, somewhat useful, or not useful, by checking the appropriate box.

Activity	Participated?	Very useful	Somewhat useful	Not useful
1. Did your child visit the kindergarten classroom?				
2. Did you visit the kindergarten classroom?				
3. Did you meet with a kindergarten teacher (not necessarily your child's teacher)?				
4. Did you meet with your child's kindergarten teacher?				
5. Did you meet with the elementary school principal?				
6. Did you participate in elementary schoolwide activities (e.g., spring programs, bingo night)?				
7. Did you go on a tour of the school?				
8. Did you talk with parents of your child's classmates?				
9. Did you attend a workshop for parents?				
10. Did you attend the school's kindergarten registration?				
11. Did you attend an orientation for kindergarten?				
12. Did you talk with your child's teacher or transition coordinator about your child going to kindergarten?				
13. Other (Please specify.)				

Are there any other activities you would like to see offered for families to prepare children for kindergarten? If so, please describe them.

Figure A18. An example of a Transition Activities Questionnaire for Parents.

Successful Kindergarten Transition: Your Guide to Connecting Children, Families, and Schools by Robert C. Pianta, Ph.D., and Marcia Kraft-Sayre, L.C.S.W. © 2003 Paul H. Brookes Publishing Co., Inc.

114

Transition Activities Questionnaire for Kindergarten Teachers, Fall (page 1)

Name: _____

You may have completed a similar questionnaire last spring. This questionnaire relates specifically to transition activities at the beginning of kindergarten. A number of practices are listed that might facilitate children's transition to kindergarten. For each activity, please indicate whether you participated in the activity. If you participated, please indicate by checking the appropriate box whether you found the activity to be very useful for children and families, somewhat useful, or not useful.

Transition activity	Participated?	Very useful	Somewhat useful	Not useful
1. I read records of a child's past experiences or status.				
2. I met with a specific child's family before school started.				
3. I met with a specific child's family after school started.				
4. I sent a note or flyer to a child's family.				
5. I sent a note to a child.				
6. I called a child.				
7. I visited a child's home.				
8. I participated in a special kindergarten program in the summer (e.g., kindergarten camp, playground night).				
9. I held an open house for families and children.				
10. I held a "Back to School Night" for families and children.				
11. I discussed specific children or curricula with preschool teachers.				
12. Other activities (Please specify.)				

(continued)

Figure A19. An example of a Transition Activities Questionnaire for Kindergarten Teachers, Fall.

Successful Kindergarten Transition: Your Guide to Connecting Children, Families, and Schools by Robert C. Pianta, Ph.D., and Marcia Kraft-Sayre, L.C.S.W. © 2003 Paul H. Brookes Publishing Co., Inc.

Transition Activities Questionnaire for Kindergarten Teachers, Fall (page 2)

Check any of the following barriers that prevent you from implementing any of the transition practices that you think are good ideas. Check all that apply, then circle the item number(s) of those you consider the most serious barriers (up to five).

_____ 1. Class lists are generated too late.

_____ 2. The practices require work in the summer that is not supported by salary.

_____ 3. Contacts with parents are discouraged prior to the beginning of school.

_____ 4. I have concerns about creating negative expectations.

_____ 5. Funds are not available.

_____ 6. Parents are not interested or able to participate.

_____ 7. Preschool teachers are not interested in participating.

_____ 8. It takes too much time to conduct these practices.

_____ 9. I could not reach most families of children who need these practices.

_____ 10. It is dangerous to visit students' homes.

_____ 11. A transition practice plan is not available in the school or district.

_____ 12. I choose not to do it.

_____ 13. Others (Please list.) _____

_____

_____

_____

Notes

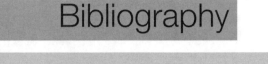

Bibliography

Adams, K.S., & Christenson, S.L. (2000). Trust and the family–school relationship: Examination of parent–teacher differences in elementary and secondary grades. *Journal of School Psychology, 38*(5), 477–497.

Alexander, K.L., & Entwisle, D.R. (1988). Achievement in the first 2 years of school: Patterns and processes. *Monographs of the Society for Research in Child Development, 53*(2, Serial No. 231).

Appalachia Educational Laboratory and the West Virginia Education Association. (1994). *Early childhood transitions: Preparing children and families for change.* Washington, DC: U.S. Department of Education, Office of Educational Research and Improvement.

Bandura, A. (1997). *Teacher Self-Efficacy Scale.* Palo Alto, CA: Stanford University.

Belsky, J., & MacKinnon, C. (1994). Transition to school: Developmental trajectories and school experiences. *Early Education and Development, 5*(2), 106–119.

Brady, S.J., & Rous, B. (1994). *"Meeting the challenge" Transition resources for parents of young children with special developmental needs. A selected annotated bibliography.* Lexington, KY: Child Development Centers of the Bluegrass.

Bronfenbrenner, U., & Morris, P.A. (1998). The ecology of developmental process. In W. Damon (Series ed.) & R. Lerner (Vol. ed.), *Handbook of child psychology: Vol. 1. Theoretical models of human development* (pp. 993–1028). New York: John Wiley & Sons.

Carnine, D.W. (1997). Bridging the research-to-practice gap. *Exceptional Children, 63,* 513–521.

Chapel Hill Training-Outreach Project and the Chapel Hill-Carrboro Head Start Program. (1987). *On to kindergarten.* Chapel Hill, NC: Chapel Hill Training-Outreach Project.

Christian, K., Morrison, F.J., & Bryant, F.B. (1998). Predicting kindergarten academic skills: Interactions among child care, maternal education, and family literacy environment. *Early Childhood Research Quarterly, 13,* 501–521.

Denner, J., Cooper, C.R., Lopez, E.M., & Dunbar, N. (1999). Beyond "giving science away": How university–community partnerships inform youth programs, research, and policy. *Social Policy Report: Society for Research in Child Development, 13,* 1–18.

Epstein, J.L. (1996). Advances in family, community, and school partnerships. *New Schools, New Communities, 12*(13), 5–13.

Epstein, J.L., & Dauber, S.L. (1991). School programs and teacher practices of parent involvement in inner-city elementary and middle schools. *The Elementary School Journal, 91*(3), 289–305.

Gelfer, J., & McCarthy, J. (1994). Planning the transition process: A model for teachers of preschoolers who will be entering kindergarten. *Early Child Development and Care, 104,* 79–84.

Graue, E. (1999). Diverse perspectives on kindergarten contexts and practices. In R.C. Pianta & M.J. Cox (Eds.), *The transition to kindergarten* (pp. 109–142). Baltimore: Paul H. Brookes Publishing Co.

Groark, C.J., & McCall, R.B. (1996). Building successful university–community human service agency collaborations. In C.B. Fisher, J.P. Murray, & I.E. Sigel (Eds.), *Applied developmental science: Graduate training for diverse disciplines and educational settings* (pp. 237–252). Norwood, NJ: Ablex.

Hightower, A.D., Work, W.C., Cowen, E.L., Lotyczewski, B.S., Spinnell, A.P., Guare, J.C., & Pohrbeck, C.A. (1986). The Teacher–Child Rating Scale: A brief objective measure of elementary children's school problem behaviors and competencies. *School Psychology Review, 15,* 393–409.

Howes, C. (1990). Can the age of entry into child care and quality of child care predict adjustment to kindergarten? *Developmental Psychology, 26*(2), 292–303.

Kraft-Sayre, M.E., & Pianta, R.C. (1999a). *Elementary school personnel contact log.* Charlottesville: University of Virginia, National Center for Early Development & Learning.

Kraft-Sayre, M.E., & Pianta, R.C. (1999b). *Kindergarten Transition Project parent interviews.* Charlottesville: University of Virginia, National Center for Early Development & Learning.

Kraft-Sayre, M.E., & Pianta, R.C. (1999c). *Transition practices menu checklist.* Charlottesville: University of Virginia, National Center for Early Development & Learning.

Kraft-Sayre, M.E., & Pianta, R.C. (1999d). *Transition to kindergarten activities questionnaires.* Charlottesville: University of Virginia, National Center for Early Development & Learning.

Kraft-Sayre, M.E., & Pianta, R.C. (2000a). Enhancing the transition to kindergarten: Connecting families and schools. *Dimensions of Early Childhood, 29*(1), 25–29.

Kraft-Sayre, M.E., & Pianta, R.C. (2000b). *Kindergarten Transition Project debriefing interview.* Charlottesville: University of Virginia, National Center for Early Development & Learning.

Ladd, G.W., & Price, J.M. (1987). Predicting children's social and school adjustment following the transition from preschool to kindergarten. *Child Development, 58,* 1168–1189.

Logue, M.E., & Love, J.M. (1992). Making the transition to kindergarten. *Principal, 71*(5), 10–12.

LaParo, K., & Pianta, R.C. (1999). Patterns of family–school contact in preschool and kindergarten. *School Psychology Review, 28*(3), 426–438.

Love, J.M., Logue, M.E., Trudeau, J.V., & Thayer, K. (1992). *Transition to kindergarten in American schools* (Contract No. LC 88089001). Washington, DC: U.S. Department of Education.

Maxwell, K.L., & Eller, S.K. (1994, September). Children's transition to kindergarten. *Young Children, 49*(6), 56–63.

Moles, O.C. (Ed.). (1996). *Reaching all families: Creating family-friendly schools.* Washington, DC: U.S. Department of Education, Office of Educational Research and Improvement.

National Education Goals Panel. (1997). *The national education goals report: Building a nation of learners.* Washington, DC: Author.

National Parent–Teacher Association. (2000). *Building successful partnerships: A guide for developing parent and family involvement programs.* Bloomington, IL: National Education Services.

Nicholson, J., Atkins-Burnet, S., & Meisels, S.J. (1996). *The Early Childhood Longitudinal Study—Teacher Questionnaire.* Ann Arbor: University of Michigan.

Pianta, R.C. (2001). *Student–Teacher Relationship Scale.* Lutz, FL: Psychological Assessment Resources, Inc.

Pianta, R.C., & Cox, M.J. (Eds.) (1999). *The transition to kindergarten.* Baltimore: Paul H. Brookes Publishing Co.

Pianta, R.C., Cox, M.J., Taylor, L., & Early, D. (1999). Kindergarten teachers' practices related to the transition into school: Results of a national survey. *Elementary School Journal, 100*(1), 71–86.

Pianta, R.C., & Kraft-Sayre, M.E. (1999, May). Parents' observations about their children's transitions to kindergarten. *Young Children, 54*(3), 47–52.

Pianta, R.C., Kraft-Sayre, M.E., Rimm-Kaufman, S.E., Gercke, N., & Higgins, T. (under review). Collaboration in building partnerships between families and schools: The National Center for Early Development & Learning's Kindergarten Transition Intervention. *Early Childhood Research Quarterly Special Issue: Partnerships in Inquiry. New Models for Early Childhood Research Collaboration.*

Pianta, R.C., & McCoy, S. (1997). The first day of school: The predictive value of early school screening. *Journal of Applied Developmental Psychology, 18,* 1–22.

Pianta, R.C., & Walsh, D.J. (1996). *High-risk children in schools: Creating sustaining relationships.* New York: Routledge, Kegan-Paul.

Ramey, S.L., Lanzi, R.G., Phillips, M.M., & Ramey, C.T. (1998). Perspectives of former Head Start children and their parents on the transition to school. *Elementary School Journal, 98*(4). 311–328.

Ramey, S.L., & Ramey, C.T. (1998). Commentary: The transition to school opportunities and challenges for children, families, educators, and communities. *Elementary School Journal, 98*(4), 293–295.

Regional Educational Laboratories' Early Childhood Collaboration Network. (1995, November). *Continuity in early childhood: A framework for home, school, and community linkages.* Washington, DC: U.S. Department of Health and Human Services, Administration on Children, Youth and Families, & U. S. Department of Education, Office of Educational Research and Improvement.

Reynolds, A.J. (1989). A structural model of first-grade outcomes for an urban, low socioeconomic status, minority population. *Journal of Educational Psychology, 81,* 594–603.

Rimm-Kaufman, S.E., & Pianta, R.C. (1999). Patterns of family–school contact in preschool and kindergarten. *School Psychology Review, 28*(3), 426–438.

Rimm-Kaufman, S.E., & Pianta, R.C. (2001). An ecological perspective on the transition to kindergarten: A theoretical framework to guide empirical research. *Journal of Applied Developmental Psychology, 16*(1), 117–132.

Rimm-Kaufman, S.E., Pianta, R.C., & Cox, M.J. (2000). Teachers' judgments of problems in the transition to kindergarten. *Early Childhood Research Quarterly, 15*(2), 147–166.

Rosenkoetter, S.E. (1995). *It's a big step: A guide for transition to kindergarten.* Washington, DC: Bridging Early Services Transition Task Force.

Rosenkoetter, S.E., Hains, A.H., & Fowler, S.A. (1994). *Bridging early services for children with special needs and their families: A practical guide for transition planning.* Baltimore: Paul H. Brookes Publishing Co.

Thorndike, R.L., Hagan, E.P., & Sattler, J.M. (1986). *The Stanford-Binet Intelligence Scale* (4th ed.). Chicago: Riverside Publishing.

Turnbull, H.R. (1998). Positive behavioral supports and IDEA. *TASH Newsletter, 23/24,* 8–9.

U.S. Department of Health and Human Services, Administration on Children, Youth, and Families, Head Start Bureau. (1988). *Transition from preschool to kindergarten.* Chapel Hill, NC: Chapel Hill Training-Outreach Project.

U.S. Department of Education. (1994). *Strong families, strong schools.* Washington, DC: Author.

U.S. Department of Health and Human Services, Administration on Children, Youth and Families, Head Start Bureau. (1996). *Effective transition practices: Facilitating continuity: Training guide for the head start learning community.* Washington, DC: Aspen Systems Corporations.

Index

Page references followed by *f* or *t* indicate figures or tables, respectively.